SHELL CARVING

SHELL CARVING

History and Techniques

Carson I. A. Ritchie

SOUTH BRUNSWICK AND NEW YORK: A. S. BARNES AND COMPANY
LONDON: THOMAS YOSELOFF LTD

© 1974 by A. S. Barnes and Co.

A. S. Barnes and Co., Inc.
Cranbury, New Jersey 08512

Thomas Yoseloff Ltd.
108 New Bond Street
London W1Y OQX, England

Library of Congress Cataloging in Publication Data

Ritchie, Carson I   A
   Shell carving; history and techniques.

   Includes bibliographical references.
   1.   Shellcraft.   I.   Title.
NK8643.R57   736'.6   73-120
ISBN 0-498-07928-7

PRINTED IN THE UNITED STATES OF AMERICA

For my wife, Bernadine Bailey

Contents

Acknowledgments

That I have been fortunate in putting before the reader so much unpublished material, particularly in the form of shell carvings which have never been photographed before, is because many people have gone out of their way either to secure new photographs for me or to allow me to have part of their collection photographed. I should like to thank particularly Mr. Woodward, for allowing me to examine his treasures and have many of them photographed, Hugh M. Moss, for a similar courtesy, and Messrs. Friedlein, of Natural Products, Kudu House, 718 Old Ford Rd., London, E. 3. for a like kindness. Messrs. Hany M. Qumsiyah and Brothers generously put at my disposal not merely photographs of their work but were prepared to talk about the secrets of their age-old art, something which is not very common among craftsmen, even in England. Mr. Matthews of the London Library has, as always, been very kind. Mr. T. C. Mitchell of the Western Antiquities, the British Museum, and Mr. C. L. Blackmore of the Tower Armouries were particiularly helpful. My wife read my typescript and procured some of the photographs for me, as well as assisting the progress of the book in many other ways. My particular thanks are due to the two ladies who helped me with translation, Lady Crawley Boevy and Mrs. Eva Light.

SHELL CARVING

1

Faces of the Gods: Mexican Shell Mosaics

NO SHELL CARVINGS HAVE ATTRACTED MORE attention—and more controversy—than those made in North America. Paradoxically, the Aztecs, Mayas, and Toltecs were content to ignore the brightest treasures of the Caribbean and Pacific, the Helmet Shells. They also made a very sparing use of tortoiseshell. Juan de Grijalva, who explored the coasts of Mexico and Yucatan in 1519 and 1520, noticed Indians with shields of burnished tortoiseshell which shone like gold. At the other end of the period of exploration in American history, Exquemelin and his buccaneer shipmates were attacked in the Caribbean by Indians wearing false beards of tortoiseshell. Between these two incidents, the occurrence of tortoiseshell, either in literary references or as material finds, appears to be totally wanting. In spite of the fact that Friar Bernardino de Sahagun, the Spanish chronicler, assures us that the Aztec lapidaries were so clever that they could smell precious stones buried deep in the ground, so long as they were down wind of them, they worked neither in cameos nor in tortoiseshell, though both lay on their doorsteps.

The reasons for this neglect were in part geographic. Only on the coast of Campeche, particularly near Jaina, did Mayan shell carving achieve particular distinction. There the Mayas sculptured large areas of shell into bas-reliefs, cutting out cloisonnés which were inlaid with apple-green jade. Elsewhere, the Maya probably trembled before the

seaborne raids of the Caribs. The latter, a ferocious race of man eaters (from whom we derive our own word *cannibal*), were great canoe builders and seafarers. They would descend unexpectedly on the Mayan coast, club as many of the inhabitants as they could catch with their wooden swords, and make a picnic of their flesh on the beach before sailing back to the Antilles. The terrors of the shore may have discouraged the Maya from exploring its treasures, while trade interruptions prevented enough bartered shell from reaching the interior to allow a flourishing art to become mature.

Although the Aztecs never subjected the coastal kingdoms to the full weight of their military hegemony, their grip on the coast dwellers was sufficiently strong to ensure regular supplies of shells as tribute. The *Codex Mendoza*, an Aztec record of 1521 listing the taxes paid to Montezuma, mentions 800 shells as part of the contributions. The limited scope of Aztec shell carving may be due to cultural derivation. Aztec records themselves are clear on this point, alluding to shell craft as an art which had been introduced to them by their culture hero, Quetzalcoatl. I feel that it can be no accident that on both sides of the Pacific shell artists set nacre plaques on a wooden base with the help of resinous gummy compounds. The Aztecs, then, may have preferred mother-of-pearl to other shells because it was this kind of shell to which they had been introduced originally. As a

Maya pendant from Jaina, now lacking its former jade inlay.

sculptor who knows how hard it is to find new ideas in art, I find it a little difficult to believe that mosaic should have been spontaneously invented in different parts of the world.

To the pearl shell, which had perhaps formed the principal kind of mosaic to which the Aztecs were originally introduced, was added the thorny oyster or *spondylus americanus*. This bright red bivalve, with its many extruding spines which make it look like a pincushion, provided the red portions of the mosaics made from shell and precious stones by the Maya and Aztecs. The high price set upon this shell by the Aztecs can be seen from the fact that they were prepared to use it even in a badly damaged condition. I inspected the other day one of the most famous of all the Aztecs mosaics, the helmet which is one of the great treasures of the British Museum (Ethnography) in Burlington House, London. I had been looking rather closely at a red tessera of mosaic, which still showed clearly the ribbed lines of the outside of a thorny oyster, when I noticed to my astonishment that this tessera, and many others, were "scabby," that is, they had been bored by worms during the shell's lifetime. Damage of this sort to a shell would nowadays means that it was rejected out of hand by a craftsman as not worth carving. Out of curiosity I counted

all the scabby tesserae which I could see. Although the helmet had lost many of its tesserae there were no fewer than fifty-two worm-eaten ones still in place. I could only conclude that thorny oysters must have been very desired, and in very short supply, for such shells to be used, especially as there was nothing else about the helmet that suggested that cost must be counted. On the contrary, the other colors were made from expensive materials, such as turquoise and malachite.

Why particular colors of shell were chosen for the Aztec mosaics is still something of a mystery. No doubt, as in the case of North American wampum, that mosaic strung on threads, every color had a symbolic association. Then the needs of realism had to be served. A dead white shell was necessary to produce the teeth of the animals which entered largely into the existing mosaics, or of the grinning skulls which provided the horrific aspects of art necessary to titillate the palate of a people who ate the flesh of children as a snack between meals. Animals with inlaid shell teeth are so common that a standard, stylized shape of teeth was evolved by lapidaries for just this purpose. This was a technique also used in the South Sea Islands. The conch shell might have provided some of the white necessary for this purpose; if so, it seems strange

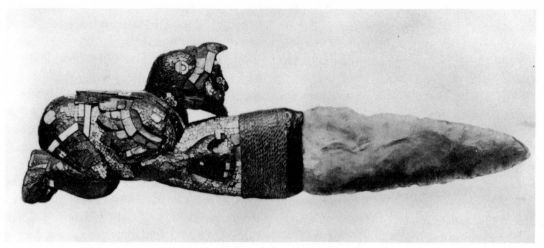

Aztec sacrificial knife with mosaic handle. Courtesy British Museum, London.

Aztec sacrificial knife with a chalcedony blade and a handle of wood inlaid with shell in four different colors: white, pink, purple, and orange, together with iridescent mother-of-pearl. Turquoise and malachite are also used for the mosaic. The figure on the knife handle represents an Eagle Knight, one of the Aztec military orders. It was with a knife of this sort that the Aztec priest sacrificed his human victim by cutting out the victim's heart. Note how practical the design of this weapon is. The mosaic has been moved back for a good distance from the blade to allow massive lashings which would enable the sacrificer to get a good grip on the handle. Lashings, unlike mosaic, would not become slippery with blood. Courtesy British Museum, London.

that the pink part of the conch was ignored. Perhaps the reason was that conch pink fades. Nacre was used for the gleaming whites of eyes in masks, while a golden shell of an indeterminate color added a rich amber.

Some of the shells used in mosaic had strong religious associations. For example, some of the tribute shells which the Aztecs lovingly inlaid with jade and carved with designs were identified by the Spaniards, into whose hands they fell as *venericas*, shells which in the Old World had been associated with the goddess Venus because of their supposed resemblance to the female sexual organs. The whole personality of the culture hero of the Toltec, Maya, and Aztec civilizations, Quetzalcoatl—the originator of shell carving and lapidary work in Mexico—was steeped in associations with shell. He never became the patron saint of lapidaries, perhaps because he was already patron god to many other arts, but he had emerged, fully formed, from a shell. He built himself four fasting houses, corresponding to the four quarters of the heavens, the second of which was decorated with "red mussel shells," the fourth with "white mussel shells." Little wonder that he was supposed to dwell in a palace built from shells, that his insignia included a shield with a band of sea shells and a neckband with golden sea shells, or that his temples were decorated with shells, such as that in Teotihuacan, which is sculpted alternately with univalves and bivalves. In addition, he is often portrayed sitting on a shell or represented symbolically by the section of a conch shell.

No doubt the house of Quetzalcoatl looked like the temple built by the Toltecs in Tula, in which, says the Spanish writer of Conquest times, Friar Bernardino de Sahagun, "The southern hall had the walls of divers marine shells, and in place of any other carving, they had silver, which was put together so nicely with the shells that the joints were not visible. The fourth hall had the walls made of colored jasper and shell, put on in a very ornamental manner." In fact, Sahagun had no hesitation in attributing to the Toltecs the development of the lapidary and shell-carving arts which were to make up the famous mosaics. "The Tultecas," he writes, "were careful and thorough artificers. Whatsoever they put their hands to, everything they did, was very good, elaborate, and graceful, as for example

the houses that they erected, which were very beautiful and richly ornamented inside with certain kinds of precious stones of green color as a coating."

By the time the first Europeans laid sight on the Mexican mosaics, their scope had dwindled from the decoration of temples and palaces to much smaller objects. Work was concentrated on idols—which were often of almost architectural size, such as the one noticed by Bernal Diaz in the principal pyramid of Mexico City: "stuck all over with much gold, many pearls and seed pearls, cemented to it with a paste made by the Indians from a sort of root," on crowns and headbands, helmets, masks, shields, knives, and blowpipes, scepters, ear ornaments, nose ornaments, breast plates, bracelets, and anklets.

Besides using shells in mosaic, the Aztecs, like the Maya, had inlaid precious stones directly into shells. Entries in the catalog of treasure sent to Spain from Mexico refer to such shell carvings as:

A shell like *venerica*, set in gold with a green stone in the center. A large shell, set in gold, with a face of green stone, and some blue and yellow little stones around the neck.

Two *venericas*, one purple and the other yellow, each one set respectively with green stones in the center, and other blue ones round it, set in gold.

Another with white *venerica*, set in gold, having some blue and red eyes, the one inserted in the other.[1]

Travelers from Spain had never seen anything so fine as the Aztec lapidary work. Although mosaic was flourishing in Europe at the time of the Renaissance, and Italian mosaicists even introduced it to India, the mosaics being made were large ones. No one remembered the small mosaics of precious stones set in wax, which had been made as Byzantine icons, except a few collectors, such as Clement VII, into whose collection passed many of the Aztec mosaics presented to Cortez. Contemporary accounts of the impression made by the mosaics also reveal that they may have looked somewhat different from the way they do now. Peter Martyr, a well known writer of the Renaissance, was shown over

---

[1]"Report of the Gold, Silver, Jewels, and Other Things That the Proctors of New Spain Carry to His Majesty," 1525, H. Saville Marshall, quoted in Contributions from the Museum of the American Indian, Vol. VI New York: Hege Foundation, 1922.

Aztec wooden helmet covered with a mosaic of red pecten shell, mother-of-pearl, turquoise, malachite, and possibly another type of pink shell, set with vegetable cement. The original design incorporated two twining serpents. Courtesy British Museum, London.

a collection of Aztec lapidary work sent to Spain in 1522 by Juan de Rivera, who had himself recently arrived from Mexico. A young Aztec slave who accompanied him helped to explain the purpose of the precious objects. "We also admire the artistically made masks," Martyr wrote. "The superstructure is of wood, covered with stones, so artificially and perfectly joined together that it is impossible to detect their line of junction. They seem to the naked eye to be one single stone." A glance at any specimen of Aztec mosaic today will reveal the existence of wide cracks between the tesserae. Martyr's statement suggests that originally they may have been grouted with a cement colored to blend in with the pieces it joined. This procedure would be in keeping with the technique of Western mosaic making, in which, from the earliest time, "it was common practice to tint the plaster that pushed up between the tesserae, so that the design would not be obscured by the criss-crossing white lines."[2]

[2]P. B. Hetherington, *Mosaics,* (London: Paul Hamlyn, 1967), p. 27.

When the Spaniards arrived in Mexico the spirit of Quetzacoatl still inspired the Mixtec lapidaries living in Aztec territory at Azcapotzalco, near the Aztec capital of Tenochtitlan. They had a millenial tradition of craftsmanship, and beautifully fashioned shell and jade masks of their crafting made in the early centuries of the Christian era still exist. "In a town called Azcapotzalco, three miles from the capital Mexico," writes Bernal Diaz, "There were a great number of lapidaries . . . even the best goldsmiths of Spain could not help admiring their work. Then for working precious stones and jades there were other great artists." From other parts of Mexico, such as the modern provinces of Vera Cruz, Oaxaca, and Western Chipas, Montezuma obtained mosaic work by tribute and barter.

Lapidary work was not merely a means of livelihood to the Aztec craftsman, it embraced a tradition of conduct which affected every action in a man's life. A sketch in the *Codex Mendoza* shows a lapidary instructing his apprentice, who is also his son. In one hand he holds an elaborate piece of inlay work, in the other a flint knife. It was with flint blades (such as the famous chalcedony sacrificial knife, now in the British Museum, (Ethnography), Burlington House, London) that the lapidaries scraped down their shell, nacre, turquoise, lignite, and even jade. All these substances are softer than chalcedony. The son listens intently to his father's words (after all, this is happening five hundred years ago) and with the help of Friar Bernardino's account it is not difficult to reconstruct what they were.

"Attend to your trade and spend your time in virtue. Idleness is the root and mother of vices, such as slander and tale-bearing. Avoid minor offenses for fear they lead you into more serious misdeeds—such as drunkenness and theft. Reverence the gods of the lapidaries, such as Macuilcalli, the deity who wears a jewel made from a round and wide marine shell round his neck. Cut your shells and precious stones by means of emery and with an instrument of tempered copper. Carve them out with a little tube of copper. Scrape them smooth with a flint knife, such as the one I hold. To polish

Aztec cedar wood mask possibly representing the god Quetzalcoatl. Two rattlesnakes twine round the face of the mask and the rattle of one of them can be seen above the left eyebrow. Although little of the mosaic of this mask is in shell, the prominent part played by the teeth, which are made from shell, indicates just how essential this material was to the Aztec lapidary. Courtesy British Museum, London.

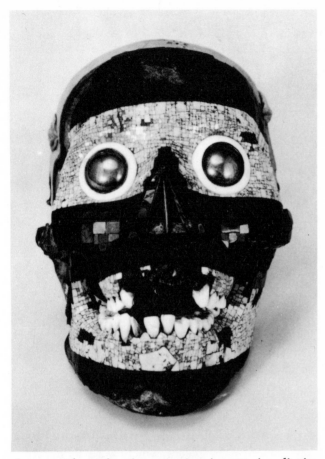

Aztec mask made of a mosaic of turquoise, lignite, iron pyrites, white shell, and pecten shell. The mosaic has been applied to a human skull, the back of which is lined with soft leather. This mask, which appears to be the best-preserved of all the British Museum masks, is eminently impractible as an item of costume. The wearer could neither breathe, talk, nor see. Once clapped over the face of a sacrificial victim, however, it would extinguish his cries and soon put an end to his resistance through suffocation. Were all the "religious" masks, as opposed to those intended as visors, in which the mouth is shielded by a drooping upper lip, originally fitted in this way, and are the open mouths and vacant eye socket merely the result of pieces of the mosaic having been lost? Courtesy British Museum, London.

them, mount them on a lapstick made from bamboo, and rub them with water and the hard stones which come from the country of Matlatzinca. Then rub them with fine sand. Put on the final polish by rubbing them with a piece of bamboo. This is hard enough by itself to polish soft stones, such as turquoises."

Mexican influence was felt to the north of Mon-

tezuma's empire, where the mound builders of the southern United States constructed beautiful shell pendants inspired by Mexican art motifs. The Indians of the Pueblos made mosaics from turquoise, bone, and lignite, but if they made elaborate inlay masks like those of ancient Mexico, they have not survived. The influence of Quetzalcoatl was also felt southwards of the Isthmus. In Peru the Chimu civilization, which flourished before 1500, made use of the copper tubular drill to create incredibly closely fitted shell mosaics in red and green segments. Shell was also used to inlay wooden figures. The Tiahuanaco culture, which flourished in the Inca confines of the Inca empire before A.D. 1000 also used shell for carving and inlay in woodwork.

No account of shell carving would be complete without some reference to the Aztec masks, which are at once the best known and least well-understood achievement of American shell art. There is no harm in referring to these masks as *mosaic*, as long as it is understood that the term *inlay* would do equally well. By their method of composition—fixing with a sticky resinous substance on a wooden base—they are much more akin to the lacquer inlays of China or Japan, or to Pacific shell inlay, than they are to the stone or glass mosaics of Rome and Byzantium. When, by an incredible act of

Chimu ear plug of dark wood inlaid with a design of a two-headed bird in what appears to be spondyl and pearl shell.

A bare-faced priest sacrifices a victim whose close-fitting visor covers the upper part and sides of his face. Codex Zouche Nuttall.

Philistinism, many pieces of Aztec mosaic work which had been stored in the Florentine Museum were thrown out in 1819, it was for inlay that they were used. They were sent to the *Officina delle pietre dure*—the workshop for inlaying patterns of precious stones on a marble base.

The lapidary began work by procuring a wooden base for his mosaic. This was sculpted exactly to the contours of the mask's face. The tesserae had to be made extremely thin to fit it; indeed they were the slimmest tesserae ever made. The method of attachment was to stick down the wafer-thin pieces of shell, turquoise, malachite, lignite, seed pearls, gold foil, garnet, and emeralds (which constituted the palette of the craftsman) to the wooden core with tacky resin, vegetable pitch, gum, or a kind of cement. In India, mother-of-pearl inlay was made in exactly the same way. A wooden base was overlaid with black mastic (a sort of vegetable gum) in which were embedded pieces of mother-of-pearl. Once the lapidary work was finished, the mask would be further ornamented by being topped with a crown of feathers.

Although masks were used for various purposes, the role of the religious ones has remained particu-larly controversial. Bram Hertz, a British collector who saved many pieces which were in hazard so that posterity could enjoy them, was told by a member of the Royal Asiatic Society, whose name he later forgot, that he had "discovered in a book" that "such masks were used in human sacrifices." Hertz, however, was unable to cite the passage concerned, and no one else has done so subsequently, which seems rather suspicious. The number of books on Aztec religion which a Victorian scholar was likely to consult is not unlimited, and it should have been possible to find this quotation—if it existed. A recent publication[3] renews the assertion that the masks were used as part of the ritual of sacrifice and worn by the officiating priest. However, the illustration of the scene of sacrifice which accompanies the publication shows a *bare-faced* priest performing the rite of sacrifice. As the author herself says, "There are many scenes of such sacrifice in the codices [Aztec books].[4] None of them, apparently, shows a masked priest. As the sacri-

[3]Elizabeth Carmichael, *Turquoise Mosaics from Mexico* (London: Trustees of British Museum, 1970).
[4]Ibid., p. 16.

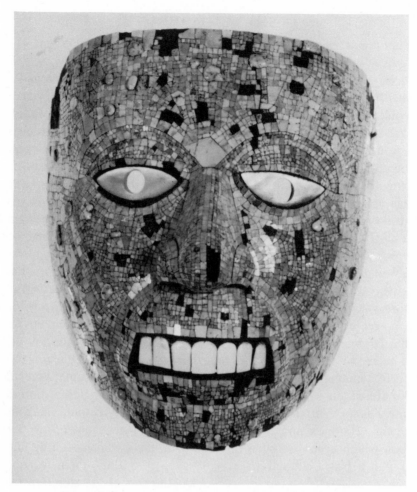

Aztec mask of cedar wood. It is covered with a mosaic of turquoise and white shell. Pierced squares of white shell appear at the temples, and the teeth are also of shell. Three features of the mask indicate it was intended to cover the face of a sacrificed victim: there is no mouth to breathe through, the mask was almost certainly "blind" originally, with inset eye pupils of lignite, and the inside of the mask was painted red. A victim whose chest cavity was being slashed open would almost certainly bleed through the mouth and nose. A red painted mask would minimize the cleaning up which would have to be done afterwards. Courtesy British Museum, London.

ficing priest had to make an incision in the left side of a victim held down on a round-topped altar of sacrifice by four other priests, and draw from his side his entire heart, it would be a feat of very considerable skill to perform this on the tough hide of an Aztec while wearing a mask with no mouth hole, and trying to squint through tiny peepholes in the eyes, All this in the mingled glare and smoke of the sacrificial fires which made the tops of sacrificial platforms on the tops of pyramids as black with soot as Victorian chimney pots. A particular mask is pointed to as just the kind that would be worn on an occasion such as this. Although this mask appears to have eyeholes, I feel myself that they are simply the spaces intended for pupils of obsidian which have since dropped out.

All the difficulties regarding the use of the mask in sacrifice disappear if it is assumed that it was worn by the *victim*, not the sacrificer. He was, after all, dressed and arrayed to portray the god to whom he was to be sacrificed. Even under the influence of drugs and religious frenzy he was probably not wholly cooperative while he was being torn to pieces alive. The blind mask clapped on his face before the sacrifice began would have the effect of preventing his seeing his executioner—like the blindfold on a man facing the firing squad. It would also partly anesthetize him—perhaps suffocate him outright, for if it had no mouth outlet he would be unable to breathe at all. It would certainly keep up the pretense that he was a wholly willing victim by stifling the cries he would otherwise have uttered. The only Spaniards who were present at the rites of sacrifice were those who acted the part of the victim. They left us no record of the details of the ceremony, but Bernal Diaz visited the great pyramid of Mexico and refers to the masks—"Indian faces" as he calls them—hanging round the neck of the enormous idol Huichilobos. A picture of a sacrifice in the *Codex Zouche Nuttall* may in fact portray a masked victim. His eyes and the upper part of his face (upon which eyebrows have been drawn) are covered with a bright-colored visor of some sort.

There can be no doubt about the functions of other masks. Just as South Sea islanders sometimes wore the decorated skull of a victim, so some Aztec priests wore a decorated skull mask slung behind them as part of their trappings. Masks were placed on the faces of the gods, as a prayer that men might recover from sickness, or laid on the faces of the dead. Masks were also worn as visors—part of the armor of a warrior. Soldiers at Chichen Itza are portrayed in the bas-reliefs there wearing just such a mask. One Spanish chronicler extolls the virtue of shields veneered with shell and precious stones. They would, he says, stop any missile, save a crossbow bolt. That the visors were not merely practicable but defensive can be seen from the fact that they did have a breathing hole where the mouth was, and the upper lip of the mask overlapped the lower, thus making a direct thrust through the mouth impossible.

It is dangerous to analyze the Aztec masks solely from the viewpoints of aestheticism or mythology. The mask makers were essentially practical craftsmen with practical problems to solve. It has been argued, for example, that a mask in the British Museum of Ethnology which is set with large, irregular cabochon turquoises represents the face of the sun god, Tonatuih, who suffered from boils. However, the snake pectoral in the case just next to this mask also contains no fewer than thirteen large, irregular turquoises set *en cabochon*. In fact, all the mosaics with any turquoises in them contain some cabochon turquoises, those with a round, irregular, and upstanding surface. Even some of the turquoises on the mask of Tonatuih which are supposed to represent boils have actually been flattened on top. It is not difficult to reconstruct this use of round and flattened turquoises, if the problem is looked on with the practical eye of the craftsman. In order to obtain tesserae for the mosaics, many turquoises were broken up with a pestle and the resulting fragments ground smooth. These are the flat tesserae. The cabochon turquoises on the other hand are "The stone that they call round turquoises," as Friar Bernardino says. These must have been naturally round, small turquoises. Instead of flattening them down, or flattening all of them down, the mosaicist simply flattened their base sufficiently to allow them to adhere to the mask and left the rest of the stone upstanding. By doing this the lapidary had achieved three practical ends. He had given the customer full value, because instead of getting nothing but flattened tesserae he was being given some thick ones as well, which were double in value. He had made the best use of his material, without wasting any of it, because it would have been a waste of good turquoise to reduce these beautifully rounded stones. Finally, he had saved himself the time which would have been required to flatten the rounded turquoises. The craftsman could probably employ any time which he saved from his direct employment to manufacturing jewelry which he could sell for a profit.

Looking, once more with the practical eye, at the use of shell in the mosaics, and ignoring the religious and symbolical associations of shells to the Aztecs, it is possible to suggest that red thorny oyster shells were employed because, as has been already noted, they provided the red which was indispensable for the color schemes of some of the designs. These include the nasal passages of the truncated nose on the skull mask, the whites of eyes and teeth, and so on. Red was also a very welcome contrast to the blue of the turquoises, which entered so largely into Aztec mosaic. Pearl shell was probably used to add life and sparkle to a design, and also to contrast with the glowing black of lignite and obsidian—the only really highly polished stones which the Aztecs possessed. Much of the sparkle of the pearl shell has now disappeared due to the familiar process of its going "blind." Many shell inserts, even of white or amber shell, were again intended as a color contrast to the blue of the turquoises. Bands of shell surround the mouth and eyes of the Quetzalcoatl. They were also intended to cover large areas which would never normally be seen at all, as in one jaguar mosaic, where they fill the space behind the broken-off paws of the jaguar. They could also be used to repair, cheaply, areas of mosaic which had been badly damaged. This is the case in the serpent mask, where a significantly large area has been filled with a single piece of shell.

2

The Talking Shell: Wampum

ALTHOUGH THE RED INDIANS CARRIED OUT SHELL carvings in more than one form, constructing beads, pendants, utensils, tools, and weapons from a variety of shells, which included clams, mussels, conches, and abalone, these objects are for the most part of purely archaeological interest. There are one or two exceptions to this general statement. The Indians of Virginia made deerskin mantles, on which they sewed, in *marginella* shells, the figures of men surrounded by deer and circular medallions. One such mantle, obtained by English colonists in the early seventeenth century from the Powhatan Indians, appears to be the only one of its kind in existence. The other principal exception to the ordinariness of Indian shell art is the gorget of the Mound Builders. The gorgets, which have been found in mounds in the middle Mississippi valley, exhibit a variety of well-marked designs. There is a rather crude mask of a human face, possibly the earliest type to evolve, with a disk of circles within a circle which recalls irresistibly the calendar stones of the Maya, stylized birds, rattlesnakes, spiders, and plumed warriors brandishing human heads, into which they plunge weapons in a gesture of sacrifice, or locked in combat. The gorgets depicting the human figure are so strongly influenced by Mexican styles of dress, if not of iconography, that it is permissible to wonder whether here we have a distinctive North American style at all and not a direct importation from Aztec culture.

No one has ever suggested that wampum was anything but North American, though, as will be pointed out subsequently, it was also made on the islands of the Pacific. The term *wampum*, or *wampam peag*, meant, in some Indian languages, a string of white beads which were used as money. "This is the money," "wrote Lawson in 1714," with which you may buy skins, furs, slaves, or anything the Indians have, it being their mammon [as our money is to us] that entices and persuades them to do anything, and part with everything they possess . . . . As for their wives, they are often sold and their daughters violated for it. With this they buy off murders, and whatsoever a man can do that is ill, this wampum will acquit him and make him, in their opinion, good, and virtuous, though never so black before."

A wampum bead was a piece of abstract art. A

Spider gorget from a mound in Illinois.

24

*Even the most primitive tribes — such as this Digger
Indian of California — possessed some shell ornaments.*

cylindrical carving, ground completely tubular on the outside and drilled right through inside, it had a very limited artistic appeal to the white settlers. "There is no particular beauty about the wampum," wrote Wood in 1875, "Indeed when the shell is, as is mostly the case, a white one, the piece of wampum looks almost exactly like a fragment of clay tobacco stem. Its only value lies in the labor represented by it, as the white men have introduced tons of imitation wampum made of porcelain, which looks rather better than the real article, and is scarely one-hundredth part of the value, the veritable wampum is so completely extinct among many of the tribes that, if one of the natives should wish to see a string of wampum, he must go to a museum for that purpose."

However degraded by later imitations, the initial concept of wampum was a strikingly bold and original one, almost unique in the concept of savage art. For one thing, a wampum bead was a standard shape (and many standard shapes of shell art will be encountered in this book). For another, each piece of wampum had to correspond exactly to every other piece on the same string. There were different sizes of wampum, just as there were for coral beads, for example, but a piece of wampum had to be exactly like its fellows. When an Indian stretched the string of beads tight and rubbed it across his nose, if he detected just one irregular bead, which protruded more than the rest, he would reject the whole string. The Indians thus invented a completely uniform currency, long before the first uniform coins with milled edges began to pour from the presses of William III's Royal Mint. They also demanded mechanical perfection from their craftsmen, who nonetheless did not enjoy the benefit of using machinery. When all this has been said, an individual piece of wampum had no importance by itself, any more than an individual tessera of mosaic. It was essentially a piece of raw material in the hands of the bead artist. Although a great deal of beadwork has been made by savage races, it is only in the hands of the wampum maker that it rises to the state of high art.

The Indians believed that the art of making wampum had been communicated to them by their culture hero Hiawatha, or by a spirit bird. Certainly the art of making shell beads went far back into the roots of Indian art. The quills of eagle feathers and the wings of large birds had preceded the extensive ues of shell wampum before the introduction of new tools for making it brought in by the whites. Wooden wampum beads had also been used.

The principal wampum shell was the quahog, or *venus mercenaria*. The Latin term for this shell which means "mercenary Venus" in English, recalls the misuse of the currency which Lawson referred to. The clam is heart shaped, and some three inches across; inside it is colored white, with a broad purple border, like the toga of a Roman senator (whose robes were dyed with a pigment taken from another shell called *murex*.) As only about half an inch of the rim of the quahog could be used to make purple beads, they were always much more in demand than the white ones. In 1640, Masachusetts fixed the

Indian chief wearing the runtee. *Its resemblance to the South Sea kap kap is striking.*

value of wampum beads by enacting "white to pass at four, and blue at two a penny." Wampum was arranged in strings of six feet, or a fathom. Because, as has been already noted, the size of wampum beads varied, the number of beads in the fathom varied as well. Where four beads made a penny, as under the Massachusetts standard of 1640, the fathom counted 240 beads. A fathom of the best wampum would buy a beaver. Wampum went on circulating during the eighteenth century, and it was still current, alongside of silver, in Connecticut as late as 1704. Long after that date traders in the Far West found it convenient to carry wampum with them. They found that the Indians would readily accept it while they would refuse silver. One reason for this choosiness on the part of the Indian traders was that, not being metallurgists themselves, they found it difficult to determine the genuineness of metal coin offered them.

The English colonists were absolutely fascinated with the idea that they found themselves in a land where sea shells were current coin. They tried,, eagerly, to make it for themselves, apparently concentrating their efforts on the quahog, rather than on the Virginian shell called *roenoke,* the common whelk, or any of the other wampum shells, Their success was very mixed. Some of them found the shells used, such as those in Carolina, so hard that they could not cut them. Others found that shells current further north, round about New York, for example, were only to be drilled for a larger expenditure of time than the wampum was worth. "An Englishman," writes Lawson, "could not afford to make so much of this wampum for five or ten times the value . . . . This the Indians grind on stones and other things until they make it current, but the drilling is the most difficult to the Englishman, which the Indians manage with a nail stuck in a cane or reed. Thus they roll it continually on their thighs with their right hand, holding the bit of shell with their left; so, in time they drill a hole quite through it which is very tedious work, but . . . . The Indians are a people that never value their time, so that they can afford to make them and never need to fear the English will take the trade out of their hands."

Probably the Indians were not ready to communicate the secrets of the wampum-making art to white rivals. They may even have deliberately mis-

The Sioux belle wore strings of white wampum, an emblem of innocence, around her neck.

led them as to how the beads were made. At any rate, the method Lawson describes does not appear to be a very efficient one. Other accounts of the wampum-making process describe how the beads were made by first digging up the clams with a long-toothed rake. They were then broken to pieces and polished on a grindstone, or rubbed down between two rubbing stones until each bead was reduced to a polished cylindrical tube about a quarter of an inch long. Alternately the beads could be pierced first, using an Archimedean drill or pump drill. — a tool in use by the Zuni Indians of New Mexico to pierce turquoises — which are a lot harder than shells — as late as the 1880s. This drill is so efficient that one almost exactly like it is employed by modern jewelers for making beads. Next the beads would be threaded on a suitable string, such as the sinews from the leg muscle of a deer, and ground smooth between two rubbing stones.

*The finery of this Mandan brave includes strings of
wampum with alternate white and black beads.*

*North American, probably Iroquois, wampum belt with
small medicine bag attached. Courtesy British Museum,
London, England.*

In spite of the difficulties, settlers persevered with the production of wampum. The Dutch introduced methods of making wampum beads which are almost identical to those employed by the *bucatrice* or "bow women" of contemporary Naples for making coral beads. At Albany, white settlers and Indians descended side by side to the shore to collect the clams which formed the raw material of wampum. At the shell factories of Long Island the Iroquois worked all the year round at making beads, storing up shells in the summer against the winter. Many thousands of strings would change hands on the beach, where the wampum makers handed them over in exchange for the pelts brought there for barter. Meanwhile the grindstones of Albany would hum on. Albany was a particularly well-sited place for making wampum because conferences took place there between "Corlaer" (the

Indian name for the governor of New York) and his Indian allies. Some colonists, like Thomas Prince, governor of Massachusetts, took the manufacture of wampum very seriously. Prince got a charter giving him the monoply of its fabrication in Massachusetts.

As late as 1844, wampum was still being made in Bergen County, New Jersey, for sale to traders to the Indians of the Far West. Like the *bucatrice* of Torre del Greco — a suburb of Naples — who make coral beads, all the wampum makers were women. They began by breaking away the thin portions of the quahog with a light hammer. Next they clamped a fragment of shell into a tool not unlike the *main* used in Dieppe, a stick with a saw cut in it to hold the shell. When the fragment had been ground into an eight-sided figure about an inch long, it was removed, placed in a homemade clamp fixed immovably on a bench, and drilled through. The drill point was made from a piece of an old saw, ground and tempered in a candle. It was held in a shaft, the butt end of which was braced against a steel plate on the operative's chest. The drill shaft was rotated by means of a bow, the string of which was twisted once round the shaft. Drops of water fell continually onto the shell to cool it, from a vessel hung overhead. Once the shell had been drilled halfway through from one side, it was reversed and drilled from the other. These precautions were taken in case it got so hot that it broke. Once they had been drilled, the beads were strung on a wire, which was passed against the grooves in a fluted grindstone. This was worked by a foot treadle, and while the operative pressed it, she turned the beads with a piece of wood so that they were evenly ground on all sides. Once finished, the wampum was threaded on hemp strings a foot in length. The women could make from five to ten such strings a day. They were sold to country merchants for twelve and a half cents a string. "They always command cash, and constitute the support of many a poor and worthy family." [1]

Even when performed with the help of machinery, wampum making sounds like a very laborious business. Many Indians were glad to abandon their traditional methods of making the beads. Many of them bought the white men's awls. Roger Williams, and other colonists, did a brisk trade in selling to the Indians the "mucksucks" which replaced their former flint-pointed drills. The articles with which East Hampton was bought in 1648 included a hundred such awl blades.

Because of the speed with which it could be manufactured by the system of domestic industry, and because various ways of imitating wampum had been discovered, it began to be worn, not just by chiefs and great men among the Indians, but by ordinary folk as well. "Below the Sioux," wrote Catlin in 1832, "and along the whole of our Western frontier, the different tribes are found loaded and beautifully ornamented with it, which they can now afford to do, for they consider it of little value,

as the fur traders have ingeniously introduced a spurious imitation of it, manufactured by steam or otherwise, or porcelain or some composition closely resembling it, with which they have flooded the whole Indian country, and sold at so reduced a price as to cheapen and consequently destroy the value and meaning of the original wampum."

Before the destruction of real wampum, however, works of a high order had been created in it. Roger Williams, writing in 1631, enumerates some of them. "They hang these strings of money about their necks and wrists, as also upon the necks and wrists of their wives and children. *Machequoce* [is the name of] a girdle which they make curiously of one, two, three, four, and five inches thickness and more of this money, which (sometimes to the value of £10 and more) they wear about their middle, and as a scarf about their shoulders and breast. Yea, the princes make rich caps and aprons (or small breeches) of these beads thus curiously strung into many forms and figures, their black and white finely mixed together," Wampum ornaments were worn as an emblem of authority by chiefs. Pendants, masks, pins, gorgets, and runtees (circular breast ornaments suspended from the neck) were also made from it. It was buried with the dead, paid over as ransom, given away as presents, or sent to console those who mourned. Six strings of wampum was the value of a man's life, and would be paid over and accepted as the price of his blood.

The most famous use of wampum was, of course, its employment in belts as the credentials of Red Indian ambassadors, and an *aide memoire* to them when they delivered parts of their speeches. Like the Chinese, whose first writings were knotted strings, and the Incas, who also employed knotted string *quipus,* the Indians also kept records on wampum belts. Wampum was turned into a belt by being strung upon animal sinews in a particular pattern. The most usual width of a belt was seven beads, or about three fingers in width. The length ranged from two to six feet. The largest known war belt is that of Pontiac, on which he recorded the emblems of the forty-seven tribes and villages who had joined him in his war of extermination against the whites. It was six feet long and four inches wide. The belt maker began by getting ready his wampum, in various colors, his threads, which could be twisted from

[1]Quoted in Albany, University of the State of New York, New York Museum, Bulletin XLI. VIII, "Wampum and Shell Articles used by the New York Indians," by W. M. Beauchamp, Albany 1901.

North American Indian wampum belts, the top one with a shell runtee attached. Courtesy British Museum, London, England.

Delaware Indian wampum belt. Courtesy British Museum, London, England.

filaments of slippery elm, but which had originally always been animal sinews, and the sprung frame upon which the belt was to be mounted while it was being woven. The seven threads were then stretched out, like the warp of a loom, the beads slipped on, seven at a time, and each was securely tied to the threads running lengthwise. When all the beads had been tied in place, the ends of the cords were tied.

The end of the belt was now covered and trimmed with ribbons.

The figures on a wampum belt spelled out particular ideas to an Indian — or at least to the chiefs and officials who were the custodians of them, and the young people who were instructed in their significance. Major Rogers of Rogers' Rangers told his readers, "The belts that pass from one nation to another in all treaties, declarations, and important transactions are very carefully preserved in the chief's cabins and serve not only as a kind of record or history, but as a public treasury. According to the Indian conception, these belts could tell, by means of an interpreter, the exact rule, provision, or transaction talked into them at the time and of which they were the excluive record. A strand of wampum, consisting of purple or white shell beads, or a belt woven with figures formed by beads of different colors, operated on the principle of associating a particular fact with a particular string or figure, thus giving a serial arrangment to the facts as well as fidelity to the memory. These strands and belts were the only visible records of Iroquois, but they required the trained interpreters who could draw from their strings and figures the acts and intentions locked up in their remembrance."

Just how wampum records managed to be stored up for posterity, messages in wampum sent to other tribes, wampum presented to chiefs, and given away in diplomatic exchanges, without the supply ever giving out, is something which has never been explained, It is true that occasionally there are references to wampum being in short supply, so that, for example, black wampum had to be painted white with clay.

Did the signs on the wampum belt have a single objective meaning, or were they subjective, meaning one specific fact to the man who drew them up, like a knot in a handkerchief, for example? Some of the wampum figures admit of a reasonable interpretation. Two men clasping hands may represent a treaty, two hands joined together peace. Scholars, and even observers of colonial days, disagree on the interpretation of other signs. It has been said that the diamond in a wampum belt represented the council fire. Others have suggested that the Five Nations of the Iroquois were represented by five diamonds. On the Washington Covenant Belt, however, which contains a treaty between the original thirteen colonies and the Iroquois nations, the five diamonds are conspicious by their nonappearance. Sometimes the idea represented by the sign would be clear to the belt maker but obscure to a white man who could not understand Indian ideas of iconography. Thus when George Washington was sent on a mission to the western wilderness of Pennsylvania, where the French from Canada were believed to have established four posts, he found the Indians there had already formed an alliance with them. As a symbol of the treaty they had exchange "a white belt on which four houses were rudely embroidered, the representations of the posts which were to be defended, even at the risk of war." The clever diplomacy of Washington secured the revocation of the treaty, and the destruction of the belt. Had

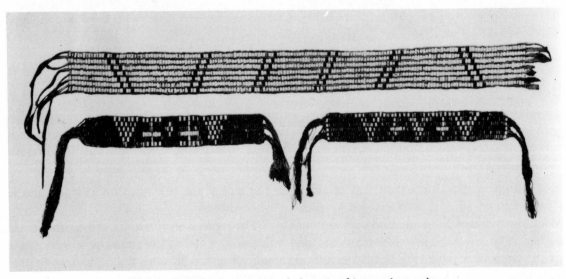

North American wampum belts of white and purple, perhaps eighteenth century. Courtesy British Museum, London.

North American Indian flat oval box and cover made of birch bark decorated with porcupine quills. The art of wampum decoration probably evolved from work of this sort. Courtesy British Museum, London.

it survived, it might have been very difficult to recognize the Indian representation of an eighteenth-century fortification.

The general appearance of a belt would immediately convey its main purpose to all who saw it, just as the symbol of war in the Scottish Highlands, the Fiery Cross, would immediately spell out its message to all clansmen who caught but a glimpse of it as it was carried through by a hurrying messenger. Thus a black belt threatened war, a red belt was a declaration of war, a white belt was a messenger of peace, and a belt covered with clay expressed grief.

There can be no doubt, at least, as to the importance of wampum in the Indian way of life. At every diplomatic exchange, wampum belts were produced by the speakers and handed over to their opposite numbers, to the sound of approbatory shouts of *Jo-Hah! or Woh!*. "With this belt," an Indian speaker told his audience," I open your ears that you may hear; I remove grief and sorrow from your hearts, I draw from your feet the thorns that

pierced them as you journeyed thither, I clean the seats of the council house, that you may sit at ease: I wash your head and body, that your spirits may be refreshed, I condole with you on the loss of the friends who have died since last we met, I wipe out any blood that may have been split between us."

Whether to the pagan Indian, who threw a string of wampum around the neck of a captive at the burning stake to save him from torture, or to his Christian brother, who patiently constructed a wampum belt dedicated to the Immaculate Virgin[2] (with a little help from a missionary priest with the spelling), the purple and white beads of shell represented the supreme embodiment of Indian art. When, in the last quarter of the nineteenth century, the last true wampum ceased to be made, it was more than the end of a chapter in the history of art, it was a sign that the heart of a great people had cracked.

[2]Musés du Trocadero, Gallerie Americaine, Paris, France.

3

Foundation of the Universe: Tortoiseshell and Nacre in the Far East

ACCORDING TO TRADITIONAL CHINESE LORE, the universe rests on the back of a turtle. This notion was so firmly entrenched in orthodox belief that there are innumerable representations, in stone, of turtles bearing columns or stelae. I have even talked to elderly Chinese who remembered buildings which had their foundation courses laid with an unfortunate turtle at the bottom of them—just so that they should not be overset. Because it had to carry so many pillars, it is not surprising that the turtle has become synonymous, in the Chinese mind, with strength and endurance. It is also the foundation of all Chinese and Japanese literature and science, for was it not after studying the back of a tortoise that the first emperor, Fu Hsi, invented writing in the form of Eight Trigrams? That the turtle had not given up all its wisdom even to Fu Hsi was shown in the sixteenth century when it inspired the Koreans to build the first armored warship and the Japanese to construct eight-sided rocks from which to rear the foundations of their castles. When an earthquake shook the land there was at least the possibility that the octagonal foundation stones would roll with the tremors, allowing the wooden castle buildings to ride on top of them until the seismic disturbances had ceased. The turtle plays a further part in architecture in that it is one of the

four animals of the quadrant, by means of which the plans of buildings are orientated.

The real attraction of the turtle to the Chinese, to whom ripeness is all, is its longevity. The people of Old Japan believed that if a turtle lived for 1,000 years it might then go on to live to be 10,000. Turtles of this age could be recognized by the trailing skirt of water weeds which they wore, and which, in Japan, earned the amphibian the name of *mino-game,* or *straw rain-coated turtle.* Turtles swam alongside the treasure ship which escorted the Seven Lucky Gods, and were the favorite pets of the fishermens' god, Kompira. Eventually, it was believed, turtles would turn into dragons, and turtle-dragons were portrayed in bronze in the Imperial Palace at Peking. Owning a piece of tortoiseshell was the nearest that a Chinese or Japanese could get to possessing the scale of a dragon. Paradoxically, however, in spite of the great respect with which turtles were regarded, it was a great insult in Old China to call anyone a "turtle's egg," or even ask someone if he swam well, or whether he liked the water. This was because the father turtle is not in evidence when his young are born and the Chinese assumed that all turtles were born illegitimate—for why else should their fathers disown them?

A large part of the respect shown to tortoiseshell

Chinese nest of lacquer boxes of the fourteenth or fifteenth century, inlaid with mother-of pearl. Courtesy Victoria and Albert Museum, London.

in China stemmed from the fact that it was employed to produce oracles which, it was believed, would foretell the future. In the Shang-Yin dynasty, eighteen hundred years before Christ, pieces of tortoiseshell would be touched with a red hot bronze rod. Once it became sufficiently heated, the shell would crack. The patterns of the cracks would then be interpreted in the light of former oracle shells, and the future predicted.[1] The prophecy (perhaps it would be better to call it an omen) which the shamans examining the shell formulated would then be inscribed on its surface with a bronze stylus.

Hitherto the Chinese had used crude reed pens and scraps of bamboo for their writing. The need to classify the oracle shells in a script which would not rub off led them to develop a special kind of writing, called *shell and bone writing,* quite different from scripts of the past. This practice was to have a profound influence on Chinese art. As well as inventing a new script, the Chinese had also discovered how to engrave tortoiseshell.

There was another reason why shell should be regarded as a treasure in China. Originally, Chinese money had been shells—cowries, and even today every time a Chinese or Japanese writes the word *money* or any of the hundred of words associated with it they have to use the shell radical, thus em-

[1]One Shang emperor consulted the oracle to discover which of his many ancestors was inflicting him with a violent toothache.

Octagonal lacquer box inlaid with mother-of-pearl. Chinese, of uncertain date. Courtesy Victoria and Albert Museum, London.

Japanese sixteenth-century cabinet of black lacquer inlaid with mother-of-pearl. Probably made for the export market. Victoria and Albert Museum, London.

Sixteenth-century Japanese lacquer cabinet. Courtesy Victoria and Albert Museum, London.

phasizing the connection between riches and shells.

Tortoiseshell and horn workers were often one and the same. These craftsmen had evolved an elaborate technique for working their raw material which was recorded just as horn working began to lose its former importance in the first quarter of the twentieth century. Horn lanterns would be made in this way. The horns of sheep and goats were boiled down until the different layers of horn could be separated from one another with a sharp tool. The horn layers were then allowed to simmer slowly in a pan of water until they became soft, transparent, and ready to be pressed. Now they were molded in a simply constructed press of hard wood and preheated metal plates. When the plates emerged from the press their edges were carefully scraped down with a metal rasp so that they would fit well into one another. The seams where two leaves met were now moistened and welded together by pressure from a hot iron. Finally, the completed lantern was polished with a mixture of lime and coal dust spread on a soft woolen rug.

By the nineteenth century, horn and tortoiseshell work was being carried on side by side in Canton. Elaborate designs of similar handiwork were in use because the two substances are closely related in quality and methods of work.[2]

The tortoiseshell used, called *tai mei*, came principally from the Loggerhead Turtle, a native of the Malay Archipelago and the Indian Ocean. It was brought to Canton from Singapore, the principal market. Some turtles, however, were caught in Chinese waters by a method invented by the Chinese. A *remora*—a fish with a very tenacious sucker on the back of its head, which enabled it to grip tightly to any object, such as a ship, and be carried along with it—was used to capture the turtles. The fisherman would procure several good-sized remoras and fasten small iron rings to their tails, with strong, thin lines of considerable length attached to the ring. He would then look out for a basking turtle and turn loose on it several remoras. If any tried to attach themselves, not to the turtle, but to the bottom of the sampan, they would be gently prodded off with a bamboo pole. Once they had latched on to the turtle the lines would be hauled

Sixteenth-century Japanese lacquer cabinet with mother-of-pearl inlay. *Courtesy Victoria and Albert Museum, London.*

in, while the turtle struggled helplessly. The remora could not be pulled away from its prey without injury to the fish, but it could detach itself instantly if it wished. It was persuaded to let go by hauling it out of water, with the turtle, and was then dropped back again, ready to effect another catch.

The fashionable color of tortoiseshell in China, was quite different from what was in demand in Europe, which suited the tortoiseshell merchants, because they could divide the catch and send to China *heads* or carapaces in the Chinese taste. This showed a preference for a shell with light and dark spots which touched one another, and for a similar pattern on both sides of the plate. The Chinese craftsman tended to avoid plates which were red rather than black in color, which had few white spots, and which were mottled rather than spotted. If a Chinese merchant could obtain a really light-colored carapace—what was called in the trade a *white head*, he was prepared to pay a very high price for it. Marginal pieces, called *feet* or *noses*, were also in great demand in China.

The tortoiseshell craftsman of Canton—like the itinerant jade carver—was not always tied to a bench. Often he could be seen sitting beside a charcoal brazier, in which he would heat the pincers with broad, smooth blades with which he welded

[2]Stephen W. Bushell, *Chinese Art* (London: Victorian: Albert Museum, 1926).

Box for documents, of lacquer and inlaid with shell. Japanese, late seventeenth century. Courtesy Victoria and Albert Museum, London.

Japanese box in four tiers, of lacquer inlaid with mother-of-pearl. Tsunayoshi period, 1681–1708. Courtesy Victoria and Albert Museum, London.

shell. The Japanese islands were at the extreme northern range of the green or caret turtle, while the hawksbill was also more at home in tropical waters. In summer, however, they would make their way along the Kuro-shiwo, the Japanese Gulf Stream which begins between Luzon and Formosa and reaches northeastward to the islands of Kiushiu, Shikoku, and Honshu. The southwest monsoon also helped the turtles to reach the very southernmost part of the Japanese archipelago. Even if a Japanese fisherman did catch a turtle, he would immediately release it, after having given it a drink of sake, of which it was supposed to be inordinately fond, and telling it to report his good deed to the fisherman's god, Kompira, the parton of turtles.

"The rare occurence of the marine turtles," says Rein,, "is confirmed on all hands, and may be in-

the tortoiseshell together. Other tools which he used for working the shell included a file, chisel, and small saw. With these simple implements the shell workers made the most elaborate and deeply cut carvings: workboxes, inlay for furniture, cups, saucers, cases for chopsticks, and a variety of ornaments. The round toilet boxes, often carved with a motif of a mandarin's procession passing through a landscape of hills, bridges, pagodas and triumphal archways, and Buddhist temples, recall the designs used on ivory boxes. Perhaps Cantonese ivory carvers carved some tortoiseshell as well. The round toilet boxes were occasionally ornamented with gold. During the eighteenth and nineteenth centuries much Chinese tortoiseshell work was made for the European market. According to a Victorian observer, Chinese tortoiseshell, unlike Japanese, was never lacquered.

As early as 1874, J. J. Rein had pointed out that the inhabitants of old Japan used no native tortoise-

Japanese inro *(medicine box) inlaid with mother-of-pearl, eighteenth or nineteenth century. Victoria and Albert Museum, London.*

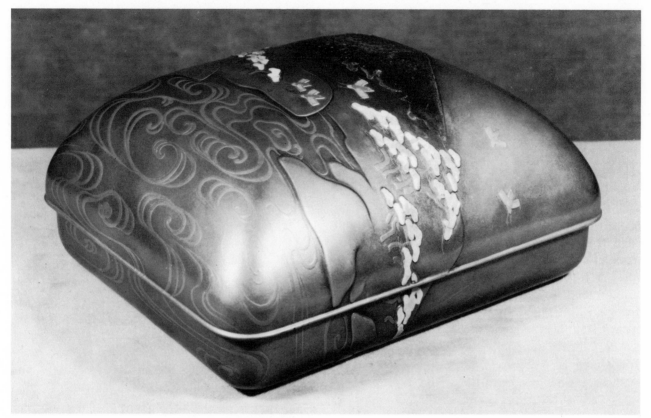

*Eighteenth-century Japanese lacquer box with shell in-
lay. Courtesy Victoria and Albert Museum, London.*

ferred from the inaccurate Japanese pictures of
them." The fresh water turtle was also never used
for shell carving, because, says Rein, "it is a symbol
of long life and happiness, of peaceful old age, one
of the seven felicities of human life. It is very often
pictured, frequently with young ones on its back, on
fabrics, lacquer, clay and bronze wares, and is one
of the most popular of animal figures. In many a
sacred temple-tank it leads, under the protection of
priests and pious pilgrims, a happy existence and
attains a great age. Here it not unfrequently happens that *confervae* attach themselves to the shell
of old specimens and develop, so that as the creature swims about they surround the hinder part of
the back like a crown of long green locks."

Much of the tortoiseshell imported for use in
Japan came from the Malay Archipelago, whence
it was brought in Chinese junks. The best quality
shell came from London, however, having been ex-
ported from American waters and the Caribbean.
By the late nineteenth century, green turtle farming

had become a regular trade in southern Florida,
where canning factories had been set up to supply
the market for turtle soup. The turtles were kept in
huge pens or "turtle crawls," consisting of fences
extending from the shore out into the water. When
a turtle was wanted a fisherman would push his
boat out among the pens. Once a turtle had been
sighted sleeping on the bottom a boy would dive
in, swim up to it from behind, and straddle its back.
The turtle would make furious efforts to dislodge its
rider but the boy would only cling the closer, catch-
ing a breath occasionally when the amphibian rose
to the surface. Eventually the turtle would become
completely exhausted and float supinely on the surface of the water, so that the boy could push the
front end of its shell over the gunwale of the boat
and enable it to be hauled aboard.

Like Americans and Europeans, the Japanese
preferred a light-amber color in tortoiseshell. From
selected pieces of shell they would make the long,
fork-shaped hairpins known as *kanzashi,* which,

together with a square wand of tortoiseshell, were thrust through the twisted braids of hair and worn by young Japanese girls of good family. Japanese craftsmen were also expert at making hair ornaments called *kogai* and matching ornamental combs called *sashi-gushi*. These were often decorated with a lacquered pattern. Rings and other articles were pressed from tortoiseshell, which was heated and then forced into a wooden mold. Tortoiseshell was also used in making *netsuke,* chiefly as an inlay.

Not less notable than Chinese work in tortoiseshell was the artistry they showed in making ornaments from mother-of-pearl. "The Japanese and Chinese have evidently means and processes for working this material which are unknown to us," wrote a Westerner ruefully in 1879, "for they give a finish and a polish to their pearlwork carvings and inlayings, which the skillful artists of the Western world admire and envy."

The Chinese superiority, which was so evident to contemporary observers, arose from various factors. They were nearer to the source of supply of

Japanese lacquer box of about 1700, inlaid with awabi shell (aogai). *Courtesy Victoria and Albert Museum, London.*

Eighteenth-century Japanese box and cover. Flowers and foliage in taka makiye of gold, silver, shell and pewter (raden) *in* nashiyi *lacquer. Courtesy Victoria and Albert Museum, London.*

pearl shell than their Western competitors. They apparently imported supplies of shell in bulk and selected the best, confident that they could always resell any quantities which they did not want to America or Britain. In 1834, it was estimated that China sent Britain 266,000 pounds of mother-of-pearl. R. Soames Jenyns has remarked; "It is difficult to surmise what these vast quantities of mother-of-pearl were used for."[3] A quantity such as that just mentioned, however, is a mere trifle compared with the probable total British import of mother-of-pearl for that year. In 1853, for example, when Board of Trade figures become available for the first time, 1,723,760 pounds of mother-of-pearl were imported. Pearl shell paid no duty coming into Britain if it were stowed loose, as dunnage in the hold. This constituted another incentive to the Chinese to export it.

At least part of the excellence of oriental shell carving derived from the use, by the Chinese, of other exotic shells, such as the windowpane oyster, abalone, and others. European manufacturers, however, did later employ some of these colorfully iridescent shells without achieving the same results.

[3]Margaret Jourdain and R. Soames Jenyns, *Chinese Export Art in the Eighteenth Century* (Feltham Spring Books, 1951).

Chinese cabinet of black lacquer encrusted with mother-of-pearl, eighteenth century. Courtesy Victoria and Albert Museum, London.

Eighteenth-century Japanese netsuke of mother-of-pearl. The surface of the shell has gone "blind." Courtesy Victoria and Albert Museum, London.

Early nineteenth-century Chinese snuff bottle. Collection of Alexander S. Cussons, Esq. Courtesy Hugh M. Moss, Ltd., London.

Chinese laque burgauté *snuff bottle, nineteenth century. Courtesy Hugh M. Moss, Ltd., London.*

The element of choice in the selection of shell is shown to be important by the fact that the emperor Kang Hsi (1660-1715) ordered that the Liu-ch'iu islands should pay a regular tribute of mother-of-pearl, because "it is remarkably pretty in these islands."

The traditions of craftsmanship in China went back for more than a thousand years. Shell workers were capable of great technical versatility. For example, they made the biggest shell buttons—which were really beads—ever constructed. These were worn on top of the hats of mandarins of the sixth grade and enabled them to be recognized instantly, even if they were in the middle of a crowded room. The types of shell carving included beads, which were made in three shapes, round, elliptical, and oval; ornaments, such as the mother-of-pearl clasp worn by mandarins of the sixth grade; boxes, with plaques of pierced, engraved, and carved mother-of-pearl forming the sides inlaid in them; models of pagodas; carved dessert plates; fans; and above all, in the export market, card counters, or *fish* as they were called in America, because they were often carved in the shape of fish. Other basic shapes included a circle, an oval with pointed ends, a flattened oval, and a square. Probably the most interesting of all the counters are those which incorporate a square or oblong shape with a frilled border cut with a piercing saw. Besides being masterpieces in miniature, counters are particularly interesting because they form one of the last frontiers for the collector of Chinese works of art. No one who has examined a counter, such as that with the initials "I.N." which I illustrate, which measures less than two inches by one and a quarter, could fail to reach certain conclusions. One, that here was work of a very high order; another, that the amount of labor required to make such a counter was considerably greater than that required to make a snuff bottle in the same material; and third, that here compression had reached its highest point in Oriental art. Nevertheless, you may still buy whole sets of counters for very much less than you would pay for a single snuff bottle, however ordinary.

An examination of just one counter will show what the European customer got for his money when he bought a set of 140. At first sight the counters look as though they were made from the shell of some naturally flat mollusk, such as the

Japanese laque burgauté *bottle made for the Chinese or collector's market about 1906. Courtesy Hugh M. Moss, Ltd., London.*

Japanese laque burgauté *snuff bottle made for the Chinese or collector's market about 1906. Courtesy Hugh M. Moss, Ltd., London.*

Early nineteenth-century snuff bottle, Chinese. Collection of Alexander S. Cussons, Esq. Courtesy Hugh M. Moss, Ltd., London.

Mother-of-Pearl and laque burgauté snuff bottle. Chinese, late nineteenth century. Courtesy Hugh M. Moss, Ltd., London.

Japanese nineteenth-century writing table, inlaid with shells in a design of the Shell Game, a contemporary indoor pastime. Courtesy Victoria and Albert Museum, London.

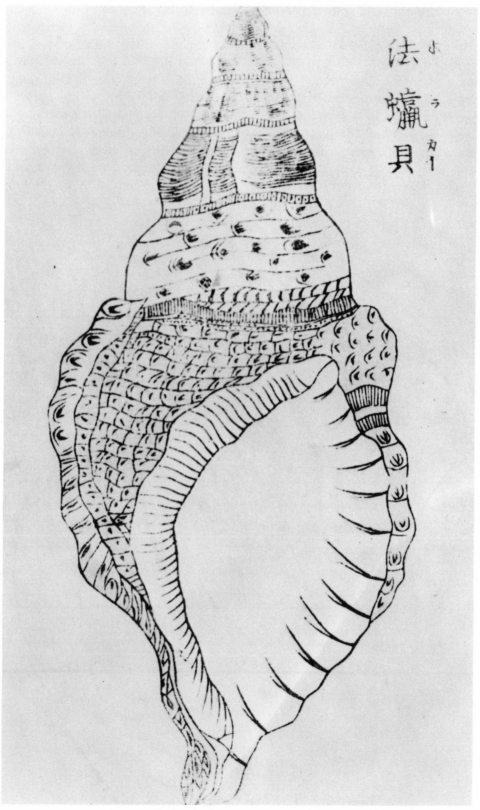

Triton's Trumpet Shell, from a nineteenth century Japanese book on conchology. Photographs courtesy Stella Mayes Reed.

windowpane oyster. Examination, however, reveals that they are too thick to be made from this shell, while they seem too large and iridescent to be made from anything other than mother-of-pearl, laboriously sawed into thin sheets. One counter in my collection measures just under two and a half inches by one inch. It is ornamented by a substantial border of fretwork, yet there is room in the panel on one side of it for a scene of Chinese life showing three men in a garden, three houses, a pagoda, a tree, flowers, plants, and rocks. The details are so miniscule that they can only be appreciated properly by examination under a 25 X magnifying glass. The carving of the eye of one of the figures is so small that it would take several such eyes to cover a pin head. The hatching of the background in these pictures is not visible to the eye of the beholder. Only when it is examined under a magnifying glass do the individual strokes reveal themselves.

Scratch carvers must have been endowed with extraordinarily good eyesight, or have done their work with the help of a magnifying glass. They

Stylized phoenix in mother-of-pearl. Shapes such as these have been current in Chinese and Japanese art from the most ancient days to modern times.

Hiroshige I's woodprint of a catalogue of shellwork made by a dealer at Asakusa, Okuyama, Japan. Nineteenth-century Japanese. Courtesy Victoria and Albert Museum, London.

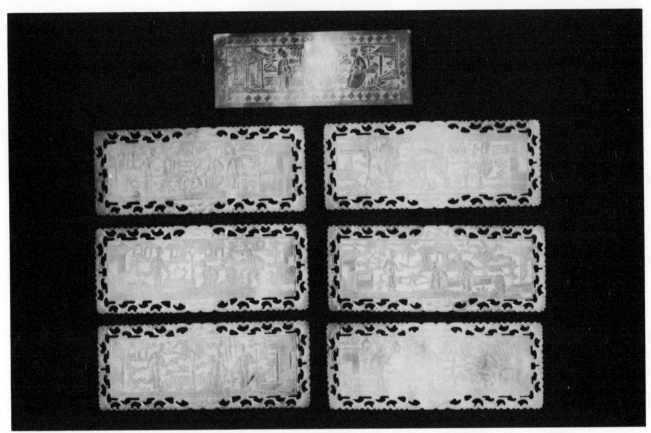

Early nineteenth-century Chinese card counters, probably made in Canton. Courtesy author's collection. Photograph courtesy Stella Mayes Reed.

used at least one European style tool, the metal compass, with which they scribed a blank circle in the middle of the counter, on which the player might note down a number. The elaborate borders appear to have been drilled and cut out with a fretsaw. The engraving seems to have been cut with a burin or graver.

The designs used on counters are particularly interesting. There is the motif of the double bird—usually two pigeons. The carp also appears, while rude pagodas are incised on some counters. There is a good deal of floral ornament, and on the square or oblong counters, many genre scenes. Very many of the counters bear the initials, crests, or coats of arms of the owners. These counters must have been made to a special order. Occasionally the lacquer box which contained them has survived. One in the Woodward Collection contains a ticket which reads *Belonging to the Box. 160 Fish, 40 Square, 29 Round Counters, 1835.*

The date indicates the period when most of these counters were made. Large numbers of counters were needed, as chips, if gambling was to be carried out, and for certain card games, such as "Pope Joan," which has special boxes marked *marriage, intrigue,* and so forth, into which counters must be dropped as the game progresses. As the Chinese did not play games of this sort, these counters were intended solely for the European market. It is a striking example of how traditional Chinese designs were employed for export. As Mr. Woodward has pointed out to me, one of the designs on a counter of his first appears as the center medallion of a T'ang glazed earthenware offering dish, dated A.D. 618.

One of the hallmarks of an old Chinese pearl carving is that it has gone "blind," that is, lost its iridescence through long exposure to the light. This phenomenon of mother-of-pearl has long been known to shell dealers, but not, apparently, to museum directors, who callously expose their treasures to the light of day. The same fate has overtaken another item from my collection, a snuffbox top carved for the European market in "gold lip" from Manila, in the shallow plane carving found in some Chinese sculptures in pearl shell.

Another of my shell carvings, however, has been exposed to the light of day for hundreds of years and still retains its iridescence. It is an *inro, or* medicine box, which Japanese men used to wear in their girdles. It is made from black lacquer, which has turned to a rich dark brown with the passing years, as the acetate of iron used as pigment in the lacquer changed color. The inro shows a minature garden, with rocks and stream, in which two children are playing. The stream and the plants growing on the

rocks are in gold *togidashi* lacquer, the children and the garden in small vertical strips of mother-of-pearl. Forms of decoration such as these are characteristic of the master lacquer artist, Soetsu Tsuchida, who worked at the end of the seventeenth century in Kyoto. Soetsu believed that small pieces of mother-of-pearl, fitted together, would hold the contour of a curved inro much better than a single large piece. Soetsu had inherited this treatment of nacre inlay from his master, Koetsu (1558-1637), and he in turn could point to predecessors who had employed mother-of-pearl with nacre lacquer in a line which stretched back into the dark ages of Japanese history.

The reason why there was such a strong reliance on mother-of-pearl by the lacquer artists is important to note. Lacquer appears to have the power of

Chinese mother-of-pearl card counters in the classic fish shape. Probably made in Canton around 1835. Courtesy Woodward Collection. Photograph courtesy Stella Mayes Reed.

arresting, in part at least, the phenomenon of blindness which has been noted as occurring in nacre. This must be the reason why so many of the pearl shell inlays used in Chinese and Japanese lacquer have retained their luster. Not all the lacquer objects so inlaid have remained wrapped away in boxes for their whole lives. Some of them must have been worn constantly by the original owners, others have been exposed to the harsh glare of a museum showroom or a shop window.

That clear lacquer was brushed over the mother-of-pearl incrustation after it had been shaped and inlaid in the lacquer base, is attested by many of the authorities on the subject, especially for such small incrustations as *aogai-mijin,* where a powdering of

shell dust is applied, covered over, and then rubbed down. In the case of *somada,* thin slivers of *aogai* were let into the lacquer, and then painted over with more lacquer before being rubbed down. It seems almost certain that all mother-of-pearl would be lacquered over with clear lacquer for the following reasons: natural products, such as cloth, cord, sharkskin, hide or leather, paper, wood, and even fungus, were brushed with clear lacquer; lacquer was used to decorate mother-of-pearl and tortoiseshell, and clear lacquer could have been applied as a base for color; it would have been difficult to embed the incrustations in the lacquer if part of it had not been painted over them and subsequently rubbed down; and traces of clear lacquer appear

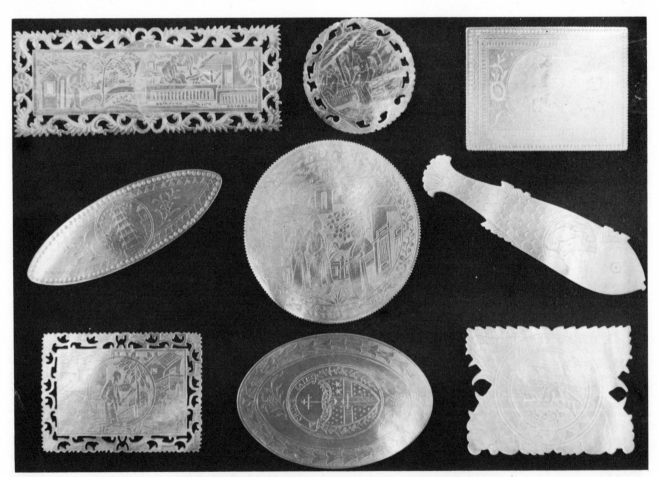

Chinese card counters of various shapes, made around 1835 in Canton. Note the owner's initials, crests, and coats of arms indicating a bespoke order made to individual requirements. This picture shows the "two pigeons" and "pagoda" designs. Courtesy Woodward Collection. Photograph courtesy Stella Mayes Reed.

Measuring less than two inches by one and a quarter, this counter is a miracle of rare device. It incorporates not merely a landscape, with foliage border, but a whole philosophy of life. The carp (left) and the butterfly (right) symbolize placidity and conjugal affection — two qualities likely to be severely tested at the card table. Photograph courtesy Stella Mayes Reed.

on shell inlays of some lacquered objects.

The fact that pearl shell and lacquer made a matchless combination, in that the one would preserve the iridescence of the other, was a Chinese discovery. Shell inlay had evolved some time during the T'sang dynasty, and perhaps it even antedated the start of the dynasty in A.D. 618. In the Shosoin, a treasure house built to house the possessions of the Emperor Shomu Tenno, and closed by his widow on his death in 756, are to be found examples of Chinese lacquer, inlaid with shell. The Emperor Su Tsung (756–62) forbade mother-of-pearl inlays in combination with amber and rock crystal because they were too extravagant. By the Sung dynasty, which ended in 1279, black lacquered boxes with

minute mother-of-pearl decorations were being produced. The inlay was fixed with copper wire, and the design was usually a floral pattern. Most workmanship of this sort emanated from the province of Kiangsi. By 1591, Kao Lien wrote that the lacquer objects inlaid with mother-of-pearl were not nearly so long lasting as they had been when, under the Yuan dynasty, the workshops of Chi-an had labored for the emperor.

During the Nara period (710–795) lacquer with shell inlay was introduced into Japan. There its successes were to be even more striking than in China, as a glance through any collection of Japanese lacquer will reveal. The choice of inlays was not unlimited, although the makers of encrusted lacquer

Lacquered screen from Indo-China, encrusted with mother-of-pearl. Nineteenth century. Courtesy Victoria and Albert Museum, London.

experimented with a wide variety of materials. Pearl shell was much less expensive than gold, silver, tin, or lead—inlay materials which were in wide use. Gold was expensive, tin unexciting, and lead and silver tarnished very quickly. Production of lacquer inlaid with nacre increased in Japan during the Heian period (795–1192). It became widely used for sword scabbards, as well as other articles, such as a book case owned by the emperor Kuammu (782-805), By 1184, as many as five lacquer masters were producing mother-of-pearl inlaid lacquer for the emperor. The nacre inlaid of Japan became so famous in China that the Chinese believed that pearl shell inlay had been a Japanese invention.

When the Ashikaga period (1336–1573) began, Japanese lacquerers turned from the large pieces of mother-of-pearl which they had favored hitherto, and under Chinese influence began to use thinner pieces of shell and powdered pearl shell. Further Chinese influence became apparent in the use of *awabi*. This was an ear shell (*haliotis japonica*) similar to the American abalone. The lacquerer

Korean cabinet of red lacquer with pearl inlay. Nine-teenth century. Courtesy Victoria and Albert Museum, London.

Chobei was the first to make use of its red, blue, and green iridescence around 1620. Then came Koetsu (1558-1637) who has been already mentioned. Both he and Soetsu believed in using small pieces of shell, but the most famous of all Japanese lacquer artists, Korin (1658-1716) is said to have reversed the process and returned once more to thicker, shaped pieces of pearl shell. I myself feel that the attitudes of lacquerers towards the pieces of shell which they used depended on the size and quality of the shell available much more than on hard and fast rules of art, which could never bind such a great and original artist as Korin. Even in a piece such as that which I have described, and which can almost certainly be attributed to Soetsu, the pieces of inlay are not *all* small. The children figured on the inro are made from quite a large piece of shell, bisected in the middle by the gap between the two halves of the inro, admittedly, but probably carved all in one piece nonetheless. Exceptional pieces of this sort, which are contrary to accepted techniques of the time, must always have been made in every period. Thus a well-known piece of lacquer, a paten, or plate, decorated with the Holy Monogram and radiating sun rays in what appears to be quite large pieces of lacquer could only have been made before the banning of Christianity in Japan, in 1614. No lacquer artist would have dared to make such a conspicious cult object after that date. Yet the proscription of Christianity comes some time before the "official" date of the reintro-

duction of larger shaped pieces by Korin.

Before the techniques of shell lacquer are discussed, some consideration must be given to the type of shells used. Apart from those which have been already mentioned, they included *omugai*, or nautilus, the top shell (*turbo cornutus*) and *trochus*, as well as the *chogai*. These creatures of the sea were all much more familiar to the Japanese than any of our beach shells to us. Unlike the average American, the ordinary Japanese never lived far from the sea, and he depended on it for a great part of his food. "The marine mollusks," says Rein, "form, in addition to numerous other sea animals, a prized and eagerly sought nourishment. Where the larger are wanting, the smaller are not despised." The Japanese learned to recognize the different kinds of shells by eating them. Like every other aspect of nature, shells figured widely in Japanese art. Edward Morse, the great American scientist who founded marine zoology in Japan during the Meiji era, found that a humble coolie, who had never had a lesson in science in his life, could unhesitatingly identify the shells portrayed in Morse's collection of Japanese art. Morse also became aware of the great part shells had played in Japanese history when he discovered the shell mounds near Tokyo which had been the food middens of Japan's earliest identifiable inhabitant, Jomon man. It is not too much to say that people in old Japan lay down to sleep at night with one ear cocked for the sound of the shell

Korean cabinet, lacquered black and inlaid with mother-of-pearl. Courtesy Victoria and Albert Museum, London.

Chinese armchair, inlaid with mother-of-pearl. Nineteenth century. Courtesy Victoria and Albert Museum, London.

trumpet which the watchmen used to signal the alarm. One blast meant riot, two fire, three robbery, and four insurrection. Shells had become charged with symbolism for the Japanese. The flesh of the *awabi* was stretched and dried before being eaten, and a proverb compared the lengthening of life to the stretching out of the flesh of the awabi. Consequently, pieces of dried awabi were frequently sent as congratulatory presents, with the implied wish *May you have a long life.*

Great skill and daring were required of the women divers, called *ama,* who dived for awabi. Their calling was a dramatic exception to the rule of old Japan that men must always lead, and women remain very inconspicuously in the background. It was the ama's husband who took the secondary role, rowing the boat for her until she had reached the diving ground, seeing that she had the half hour's rests she needed between dives, that she was able to warm herself at a fire on the beach, and get the strengthening foods she needed—abalone, sea chestnuts, and other sea foods roasted on the coals of the fire. The ama were almost the only heroines that old Japan knew. Many stories are told of the brave rescues which they performed and the swims of incredible length which they accomplished. Artists reveled in depicting their fullbreasted bodies as they poised on the side of the boat, ready for a dive into twenty-five feet of water. Their calling, which was passed on in hereditary line from mother to daughter, had developed in them sturdy legs and well-proportioned thighs and torsos. They wore a white cotton loin cloth and jacket, not for modesty, but to frighten the sharks, and the even-more-savage sea eels, which from time to time attacked them. In spite of, or perhaps because of, the fact that Japan was a country where mixed bathing prevailed and the sexes mingled freely, unclothed, in the scalding hot water of the communal bath tubs in inns, nudity never played a large part in Japanese art, with the exception of pictures of ama.

The girls, who now live mainly on the Sakishima Peninsula, began diving at the age of twelve. The lone divers, or *kachido,* worked in water from twenty to twenty-five feet deep, remaining under for from thirty to forty seconds on each dive. The divers went out in a boat and floated a wooden tub attached to their waist by a rope. They used a hooked knife to dislodge the abalone from the parent rock. An accompanied diver (*funado*) carried a net to receive the catch and was fastened to the boat by a rope. A print by Kuniyoshi of about 1833, "Low tide at Shinagawa," shows lone women divers at work. They wear red underskirts with grass skirts on top of them, a blue top coat, and a twisted cord belt. Kuniyoshi has shown the girl in the water holding her knife in her teeth, and her top coat opening out to show her breasts.

Once the abalone shells had been gathered, they were stored in reed baskets to be sent to market. When the meat had been removed, the shell was processed so as to be turned into raw material for the lacquerer. The thick, curving outer edge of the awabi was removed up to the row of holes by means of pincers, hammer, and chisel. It was also cut into shape by a fine-toothed saw. In modern times it could also be shaped by being stamped out or being abraded by chemical means.

The grindstone, which would have made light work of the wearisome task of grinding the shell smooth, did not come into use until comparatively modern times. Instead, the workman rubbed the shell on a finely grained sandstone slab, sprinkled with water, and kept on grinding it until only a thin, transparent sheet remained. These sheets sold for from two to six *sen* (a Japanese cent) according to their fineness. Polishing the sheets was such a laborious process that a man could polish only eighteen of them a day. Thicker pieces of mother-of-pearl were also ground for engraving and insertion into lacquer. The waste grindings and dust from the shell worker's floor would also be carefully collected, sieved to separate it into different grades, and put aside for various sorts of lacquer decoration.

A glance at the illustration showing the wares of a Japanese merchant of shell decorations of the nineteenth century will show much ingenious use of whole shells, which have been made into composite sculptures similar to those still made in Hong Kong. Razor shells figure as bird's tails, mussel shells as the wing feathers of storks, and *dentalium* has been painstakingly fitted together to make up stems of bamboo. Most of the wares on display are shell craft rather than carved shell, though there appears to be some mother-of-pearl

Chinese "oracle bone" from the Shang-Yin dynasty, eighteenth century B.C. These tortoiseshell carapaces were inscribed with a question in the oldest form of Chinese writings, the Chia Ku Wêng, or 'shell and bone writing.' The shell was then heated and the direction of the cracks provided the answer to the question, which might be: "Which of my ancestors is giving me a toothache?" Courtesy Gulbenkian Museum of Oriental Art, Durham, England.

inlay as well. In spite of side uses for shells of this sort—and for direct carving in the form of *netsukes*—most of the shell used in Japanese art went into lacquer. Many techniques were in use, and a glance through any collection of Chinese or Japanese lacquer will reveal just how large a debt the lacquer artist owed to shell inlay, of one sort or another.

In the technique known as *raden,* large thin pieces of mother-of-pearl were inlaid so thickly as almost to cover the lacquered ground. The pieces were shaped by being first laid on a master pattern and then having the design traced onto them. They would then be painted underneath with colors mixed with glue, and silver foil would be pasted on to the bottom of the sections to enhance the colors. Finally, any surface carving which had to be done to the shaped piece would be carried out. The workers in Buhl in France, were to adopt an inlay technique (described later) similar to this, using tortoiseshell instead of mother-of-pearl. They may have had this method suggested to them by taking to pieces and examining a piece of broken lacquer.

Another very well known technique was *lac burgauté.* This consisted of very tiny pieces of *ear shell* arranged in mosaic form on the lacquer so as to produce a diaper pattern, like brocade. The process was called *aoigai* (*ear shell*) in Japanese. Because French connoisseurs and collectors first identified the shell used in this kind of decoration, it has acquired the name *lac burgauté,* from the French name for sea-ear, *burgau.*

The forms of decoration mentioned so far were composed from carefully shaped pieces of shell, which were laid on top of the original sketch for the design, which showed through the transparent pieces of shell, traced to shape, and then cut out with a saw. In the technique known as *somada,* however, the ground of black lacquer was sown with tiny fragments of mother-of-pearl, which, says Rein,

was made up "from the mother-of-pearl dust of various degrees of fineness obtained from the waste." A very careful grading in the sizes of these irregular shell fragments was carried out when they were laid on the lacquer so that they could produce different types of effects. Like other forms of lacquer decoration, this was an importation from China to Japan. Somada Kiyosuke (1716-36) learned the technique from Chinese lacquerers in Nagasaki, and it was named after him. Another and rather similar method of shell decoration was *e-nashiji,* which consisted in dusting a black lacquer ground with powdered ear shell.

It required much less time and patience to construct mother-of-pearl inlay, to be let directly into a wood base, than to imbed it in lacquer. It is not surprising then that there is much direct pearl shell inlay in both Chinese and Japanese furniture. In Chinese work, inlay was applied both to very large pieces, such as thrones, and to very small ones, such as the present sent by the Emperor of China to Josephine, then wife of the First Consul, Napoleon. The vessel carrying this present was captured by the English, and although after the treaty of Amiens it was offered back to Napoleon, he declined. The gift of the Emperor was a model of a Buddhist temple, "picturesquely posed on the slope of a steep hill, with pavilions, pagodas, bridges, gates, and other details delicately carved in ivory, and enclosed within an ivory railing of floral design. Mandarin visitors are wandering through the grounds, or drinking tea and playing chess in the garden kiosks. The trees are made of gilded metal with coral blossoms and jeweled fruit, the birds, insects, and flowers are worked in filigree inlaid with kingfisher's plumes. There are storks shaped in mother-of-pearl, and ponds with waves cunningly worked in the same material containing clumps of lotus, ducks, and fish, with anglers on the banks."[4]

---

[4]Stephen W. Bushell, *Chinese Art.*

4

Heavenly Trumpets: The Sacred Chank

FOR THOUSANDS OF YEARS THE TORRID WATERS OF the Indian Ocean, off Tuticorin, were furrowed, during the monsoon season between October and May, by fleets of canoes, carrying teams of divers, called *parawas,* out to the banks at ten fathoms' depth in a search for the most holy shell of the far east, the Sacred Chank. If we except mother-of-pearl, the chank, or conch (*turbinella pyrum*), is the most important of all shells in art. Long before the first Roman trader, Hippalus, had sailed down the Red Sea in A.D. 45 and discovered that the regular monsoon winds would take him to India, divers were at work off the coast of Coromandel, seeking chank shells which could be worked up into religious utensils and jewellery, in shell workshops whose remains have demonstrated continuous production from that day to this.

There is a Russian proverb to the effect that no one knows how to pray who has never been to sea. Its truth is exemplified by the chank divers and their holy men — the "binders of the sea," who handed down from father to son the sacred *mantrams* or charms which had to be recited to drive away the sharks. An ancient Tamil poem, the *Maduraikkanchi,* spoke with awe of their powers in this respect. Marco Polo, who visited the Gulf of Manaar, where pearls and chanks were fished in adjoining banks (there is some affinity between the two, and no doubt chanks prey on pearl oysters) had this to say about the wizards in 1294, "These fish charmers

are termed *Abraiaman,* and their spell holds good only during the day time. At night they revoke the spell so that the sharks can work mischief at their will. These *Abraiaman* know also how to charm beasts and birds and every living thing. The divers must pay them one-twentieth of all they take."

Besides sharks, other dangers to be dreaded by the diver include headwinds, rough weather at sea, clouds, which would chill the water so much that the *parawas* would be unable to dive, morning calms which would prevent the sailing canoes from reaching their destination, prolonged rain which would flood the rivers and discolor the sea water with washed-out soil so that the chanks would not be visible on the bottom, and the presence of stinging jelly fish, such as medusa, siphonophores, the frilly *chrysaora* and the beautiful purple blue Portuguese Man-o'-War. Small wonder that the divers had to encourage themselves with copious draughts of arrack or rum before they set sail. and that they took more arrack aboard the canoes to sustain their courage as they dived. Each canoe carried six divers and one *thodai* or helper. Under the guidance of a pilot, the fleet would drift until a rich bed of chanks had been discovered. Then the canoes would anchor and each diver seize his sinker stone, jump overboard, and sink to the bottom. While the diver looked around for the few agonizing seconds allowed him for the moving brown lump which denoted a chank, or the furrowed track

61

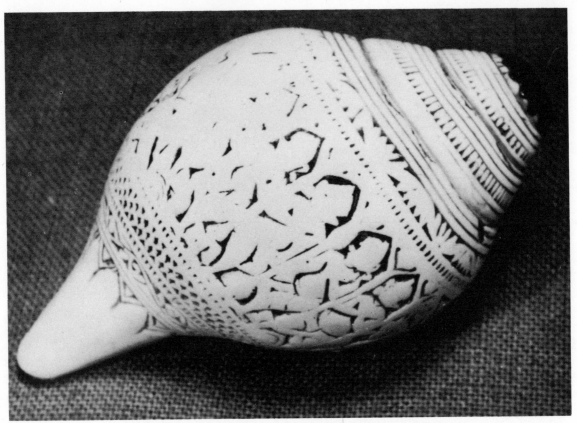

*Carved conch shell trumpet used in Hindu religious
ceremonies in Southern India. Probably eighteenth century. Courtesy Horniman Museum, London.*

which the creature had left on the ooze of the
bottom, the *thodai* would haul on the rope attached
to the sinker stone and bring it up to the surface
again, ready to be handed to a diver as he came up
from the bottom with a handful of shells.

Once the canoes were loaded, the fleet would
head back to shore, while the divers ate the meat
of the chanks they had caught, chewed areca or
betel nut, or drank a well-earned draught of toddy.
The catch was enormous; as many as five million
shells might be shipped in one year from the Gulf
of Manaar. On land the chanks would be roughly
graded, according to size, and damaged specimens
rejected. They would then be stored in a *godown*,
or warehouse, to be cleaned. "Cleaning," wrote an
English observer, "Is left to nature, which here takes
the form of innumerable fly maggots." The cleaned
chanks would next be sold to the shell carvers, who
would now begin to fashion the most remarkable
religous utensil of the east.

The chank was a religious symbol of great

potency both for Buddhists and Brahmans, the two
principal religious groups of Asia. To the latter
it was emblem of the gods Siva, Vishnu, and Krishna. Vishnu, the Protector, was supposed to hold a
chank in his hand. Shankar, the Destroyer, did the
same. The first incarnation of Vishnu, into a fish,
had been undetaken in order to destroy a giant
chank shell called Shankhasura, who had stolen the
Vedas, or sacred books of the Hindus. Krishna, in
a rather similar adventure, had vanquished the
terrible marine demon, Panchajana, who lived in a
giant chank shell and was a foe of the five orders
beings: gods, men, gandharvas, serpents, and ghosts.
The god had done battle with the watery ghoul at the
bottom of the sea and borne off his shell as a trophy.

This association wth two deities made Hindus
believe that unless they worshipped the shell at the
beginning of every religious service their offerings
would not be accepted. Brahmins made the sign
of the chank and involked it in charms, such as the
hymn from the very early work *Atharvareda,* which

runs, "Born of the wind, of the atmosphere, of the lighting, of the celestial light. May this conch protect us against danger. With this chank of the depths of the celestial deeps, of the ocean, we strike and vanquish the devouring Raksas. May this conch, universal remedy, protect us against danger. Born in heaven, born in the sea, brought to us by the Ocean, born of gold, may this conch, this gem, prolong our days."

Conch shells were blown as martial trumpets by the great warriors of the Hindu epics *Ramayana* and *Mahabharata,* just as they were by the samurai swordsmen of Old Japan, to whom the conch was the symbol of victory in battle. Whereas to the warrior the blast of the chank was a call to a war, to the priest it was a call to prayer. Brahmins used the chank to mark the hours of the four daily temple services, at dawn, noon, sunset, and night. Buddhist monks in Tibet also blew chank shells to herald the hour of tea drinking in the monastery, for it was not merely in England that the imbibing of tea had become a religious rite. The clear and mellow drone of the chank, modulated by lip movements from the instrumentalist, could be heard in the lonely caves of hermits in the mountains of China, in the crowded streets of Indian cities, where brass-mounted conches were sounded by beggars as a signal to the charitably inclined, and by the itinerant priests of Japan, known as *yamabushi,* as they proceeded along the Tokkaido or in the courts of Tibetan monasteries, where the form of the chank often disappeared beneath its rich incrustation of gold and gems.

The most valuable chanks were not those sheathed in plate and jewels, however, but those few sinistral shells which some freak of birth had wound in left-handed, not right-handed spirals, starting from the cone of the shell. This was the type of shell which the gods were supposed to carry in their hands, and the few which existed were kept as coveted temple treasures. One kept in the Sakya monastery, near Singatze in Tibet, would only be blown by the monks on the payment of seven ounces of silver. The effect of any chank shell — driving off demons and evil spirits — was of course intensified in a sinistral shell. Some were considered to be so very sacred that it was believed that they blew themselves at night.

Chanks were used to pour libations in temples,

served as oil lamps in Indian shrines, were used to smooth paper in Nepal, employed at funerals, as in ancient Mexico, and hung on the foreheads of bullocks and elephants as a good luck token.

Surely the strangest of all employments of the chank shell, however, was its use as a marriage ornament. No Brahmin virgin would think of losing her hymen unless she were wearing chank bracelets. Even nowadays the placing of two red-lacquered chank bracelets on the bride's wrist is an essential part of a Bengali wedding ceremony, which, if omitted, would destroy the legal validity of the marriage. Brides who could afford them wore several bracelets on their arms and similarly shaped anklets on their legs. These ornaments were always buried with a married woman, so there was a constant demand for more of them. Not all the chank jewelry worn in Asia was as richly carved and highly polished as that employed as marriage ornaments in Bengal. The women of Tibet, Assam, and Bhutan, who also wore chank jewelry, had to be content with plain bangles.

The craft of making these ornaments had not changed since the second century A.D., when a poet named Dharmi had written, "Spreading his knees wide, his joints loosened by the labor, does he not saw chanks into sections, his *ghee*-smeared saw murmuring the while, 'kir-kir'?"

The shell carvers lived in a special quarter of the city of Dacca, in Bengal, or as it is now called, Bangladesh, on a long, narrow street known as the Shakhari Bazaar. The craftsmen, Sankharis, were Brahmins who had been degraded for destroying a golden calf. They worshipped a special deity called Agastya Rishi, who had ridden the world of a formidable demon by cutting him up with the semicircular saw used by shell cutters. The Sankharis seldom went outside their noisome little homes and workrooms, their women never. Because Sankhari women were noted for their beauty and pale complexion, they were frequently carried off to grace the harems of licentious Muslim officials in the days before British rule in India.

The shell cutter had to begin work at a very early age so that his limbs could accustom themselves to the curiously cramped position in which the carver worked. A craftsman held the shell between his toes, while sawing away from himself across the shell with a very large, crescent-shaped saw, which was held

Conch shell trumpet from Tibet, used in religious ceremonies. It has been set in a frame of gold with encrusted gems. Probably nineteenth century. Courtesy
Horniman Museum, London.

perpendicularly over it. The difficulties of the carver's task were increased by the way in which he sat, wedged between two short posts of unequal length, hammered into the earth floor. He propped his back against the larger stake, which measured 15 inches above the ground, and pressed the shell which he was cutting against the shorter, which was 4 to 5 inches high. He had to grip the shell between his feet so tightly that it did not move. Even for an Indian, whose feet are not deformed by wearing stiff leather shoes, this was a formidable task, and it was made all the more difficult because he only had a space of 18 inches in which to sit.

The saw used was certainly the largest tool employed by any shell carver. It was shaped like a half moon, and the two tines at opposite ends of the saw were lashed onto a crossbar of bamboo. Like everything to do with the chank, the saw was regarded as a religious object. A new saw was adorned with red spots on each side of the blade after it had been sharpened — red being the propitious color of the Hindus. From time to time the saw would be lubricated with *ghee,* sacred clarified butter, and the carver would also periodically sharpen it by knock-ing the teeth back into sharpness with a chisel set in a hammer.

The carver could tell at a glance from where any of the shells stacked beside him had come. For his finest work he chose a Tunnevelly shell, selecting a size which varied, depending on whether he wished to make a narrow *churi* bangle or a broad *bala* one. Holding the shell firmly between his feet, he began by making a straight cut through it. This took four and a half minutes. Then he made another cut, parallel with the first. The bangle was now complete, save for the interior portions of the shell, the *columella* and *septa,* which had to be smashed out with a hammer. Finally the bangle would be shaped by being rubbed down with a wooden rod covered with a coat of lacquer in which sand had been embedded. The pattern was next cut in with a small file, and finally the design was colored with cinnabar which had been ground on a granite pestle with a pebble, and then mixed with shellac. The pigment was formed into a pencil-shaped stick, rather like a stick of sealing wax, heated, and dabbed on to the bangle.

Sometimes bracelets were made up from multiple

rings of shell which were cemented together. These bracelets were made to open to admit the hand by means of two spiral pins which unscrewed to let out a segment. The shell bangles, which were called *sankha,* were sometimes lined inside with plaster to make them smoother to the wrist. Filigree-bordered edges of plaster were also added to the *sankha,* and they were ornamented with silver or gold tinsel, spangles, and colored glass beads. The bangles could also be lacquered, gilded, adorned with gems, or carved with tiger's heads or enriched with ornamental incising.

Carved chank shells and ornaments made from them were among the most popular of all shell carvings, not just because the chank was the heavenly trumpet to whose tones Buddha had descended to earth, or the scepter of Krishna and Vishnu, but because to the landlocked Tibetan or even the inland Chinese, this rarity represented the mysterious ocean upon which he had never looked. Even the sound of the chank, blown in those upland valleys, must have seemed to those who heard it, "born in the sea, brought to us by the Ocean."

5

Barbaric Pearl and Gold:
Shell Carving in the South Seas

OUTSIDE NORTH AMERICA, SHELL CARVING IN THE hands of uncivilized people reached its peak on the islands of the Pacific. "We who live in an age when craftsmanship is not respected," wrote a distinguished American contributor to the domain of South Sea art, "can hardly conceive how sufficient skill can be attained to bring about such excellent results."[1]

The reasons why shell carving achieved such excellence on tiny islands where the conditions of life appeared to be inimical to any kind of leisured activity can only be discovered by probing deeply into the very complex way of life and beliefs of the islanders. It was significant that the South Sea Islands straddled the largest and richest shell region in the world, the Indo Pacific area. Within the confines of this zone were to be found shells which were completely unknown elsewhere. When, at the Great Exhibition in London, in 1851, a lay figure of an islander, wearing a necklaces of shells, was put on display, the shells were stolen — one of the very few thefts from the exhibition. Although in the Pacific they were considered perfectly ordinary shells, in London they were worth several pounds each to a collector. Even the more common shells from the South Seas were rich in color and form.

They were also frequently very large, and they included the largest of all shells, the Giant Clam or *tridacna gigas,* which had valves three and a half feet wide. It is not surprising to learn that some of the largest shell carvings in the world, the standards carried on poles in the bows of head-hunting canoes from the Solomon Islands, are to be found in the South Seas. They were made from tridacna. So rich in shells was the region that in Borneo it was possible to descend to the depths of the sea around the atolls, gaze into the many-colored smile of the Giant Clam as it opened its deadly valves to reveal a green, blue,and purple mantle, and knife it away from the parent rock, or altenatively to climb the slopes of the shore and find fossil tridacnas embedded in the rocks. No shell carver in the South Seas had to submit to working with inadequate material, as in Mexico, where very worm-eaten thorny oysters were incorporated into the Aztec masks. Thorny oysters were so abundant in the waters off New Guinea that they were worked into special necklaces which were given away as presents, and which, by custom, had to be requited by an even more valuable gift.

The islands possessed not merely the world's richest shells, but were peopled by the greatest swimmers in the world. Islanders could dive to 20 fathoms without using a weight to sink them. They could stay underwater for two minutes, then rise to the surface carrying large quantities of pearl shell,

[1]Gladys A. Reichard, *Melanesian Design. A Study of Style in Wood and Tortoiseshell Carving* (New York: Columbia University Press, 1933).

Shells were the treasures of the South Seas. The few possessions of this family include a shell necklet, hung in a conspicuous position above the wife's arm. (The husband has been to fetch a pig's head to pay the tattooer.) This rather idealized picture of life in the South Seas was drawn by a visiting Russian in the nineteenth century. Courtesy British Museum, London.

shells which measured sometimes as much as eighteen inches in width. In these warm seas, shell collecting could be carried on year-round, while the labor of women or slaves, who did all the heavy work, ensured a constant supply of raw material. In New Zealand, women were kept busy collecting oysters on the beach, or diving for them, depending on the nature of the coastline.

Shells were much more familiar to the islanders than they are to us, because they were everyday items of household equipment. Every Maori above the rank of slave shaved every day, so as not to obscure his tattooed face, and used a pair of mussel shells for this purpose. Shells were used for scrapers, tools, polishers, cups, and many other purposes. Next to fish, shellfish provided the only source of protein for islanders during times of peace, when there were no dead enemies to eat. There was no greater delicacy for the Maori than a meal of *pawa,* or abalone, eaten along with putrid potato cakes. "The two together," wrote one English traveler, "form a banquet which an Englishman could hardly prevail on himself to taste, even though he were dying of hunger." The Maoris ate great quantities of *pawa,* "from which they procure the pearly shell with which they are so fond of inlaying their carvings, especially the eyes of the human figures."

Even a cannibal feast, however, might provide the basis for a piece of shell carving. A bone from a well-hated but now digested enemy would be filed

down into a fish hook. It would then be lined with a slice of pawa shell, tufted with hair. A hook such as this required no bait. It was towed astern of the canoe, and revolved rapidly in the water. The brilliantly iridescent abalone shell flashed in the light like the white belly of a fish, and the tuft of fibers represented the tail.

Many South Sea shell carvings may have been designed for utility as well as ornament, like the fishhook. The useful purpose they were to serve would have been perfectly clear to the men who made them, though not to us. Thus the fishing floats which appear so decorative, with their wealth of shell inlay, may in fact be merely functional, and have been constructed so as to attract fish to the net by the winking play of light which the shell

Trobriand Island pump drill, with which many shell carvings were pierced and fretted. Pressure of the operator's hand alternately twists and untwists the string, forcing the drill to revolve. Courtesy British Museum (Ethnography), London.

plaques gave off. Even the wonderful shell inlays which adorned the stems of canoes may have had their purpose, because it is known that the Solomon Islanders, who used this type of canoe, used to crouch behind the high stem as they rowed up to the enemy's fleet. The flashing reflections from the shell plaques' inlay might have served to dazzle an opposing crew and deflect their aim as they threw missiles at the stem.

Shells were burned to make lime which, when mixed with betel nut, was chewed like chewing gum. Islanders learned early how to shape and grind shells by making tools from them. They were

used for every conceivable purpose, including a few which would never have occurred to anyone but a South Sea islander. The Maoris, whose taste for cannibalism had given them a good working knowledge of anatomy, used pieces of shell as operating knives in surgery. A party of Sandwich Islanders who had taken some prisoners decided that they would behead them on the spot instead of marching them back to camp. But what were they to use for knives? One of the war band silently pointed to the oyster shells which littered the ground, and in a few moments every head had been dexterously removed.

On many islands shells were the most precious objects known to the islanders because they were used as money. In New Britain, for instance, the system of exchange was based entirely on carved shells, either used in the form of large, cut shell rings or small shells pierced and threaded on strings. One island in the New Hebrides group, Matanavat, had a shell industry which was kept busy making shell beads for use as cash which the other islands would accept from white traders even in perference to silver coin.

American interest in shell collecting might be said to have come of age around 1853, when an American authoress named Amy Lothrop wrote a novel called *Speculation,* about a feckless family of shell collectors, who were always filling their ebony cabinets with shells such as Volutes, Argonauts, Stelloridians, and Carinaria Vitrea, which they bought at a high rate from fellow American collectors or imported from Europe. Long before this date the islanders had become connoisseurs in the acquisition of shells. Trading captains sailed to the Tongan Archipelago to take on a white, violet-lipped cowrie known as *ovulum angulosum,* which sold at a dollar apiece. They knew that this particular shell was not to be found in the New Hebrides and that it was so esteemed by the natives there that they would willingly cut a ton of sandal wood to exchange for just one *ovulum.* When dressed for battle the inhabitants of the Navigator's Islands wore a fillet formed from the inner whorls of the pearly nautilus. The whorls had been stripped of their external coat, so as to present an appearance of the most highly burnished silver, and were threaded on the midrib of a coconut leaf, which was tied round the head with a cord of sinnet. The

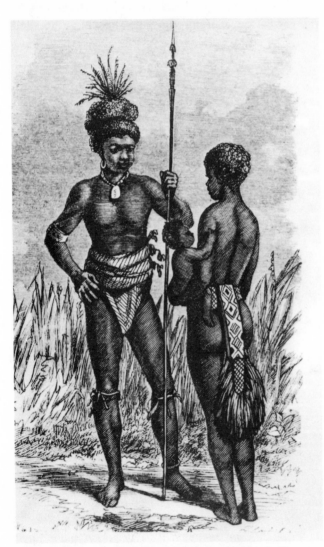

Man of Vate in the New Hebrides, with shell ornaments. From J. G. Wood, Natural History of Man *(London: 1875), p. 305. Photograph courtesy Stella Mayes Reed.*

Solomon Islands canoe house at Makira Bay, showing statue and canoes ornamented with pearl shell inlay. From J. G. Wood, Natural History of Man *(London: 1875), p. 302. Photograph courtesy Stella Mayes Reed.*

Chief mourner in Tahiti, wearing the dress peculiar to his office. It was composed of "mother-of-pearl, shell, feathers, bark-cloth, and similar materials, and has a peculiarly startling appearance from the contrast between the glittering white of the pearl shell and the dark feathers with which the shell is surrounded." From J. G. Wood, Natural History of Man *(London: 1875), p. 424. Photograph courtesy Stella Mayes Reed.*

*Maori House, showing use of human figure sculptures
with shell eyes. Courtesy British Museum, London.
Photograph courtesy Stella Mayes Reed.*

pearly nautili from which these ornaments were formed were not to be found in the Navigator's Islands; they had to be imported by European traders, from New Caledonia and Fiji, and in 1879 they sold at the high price of a shilling each.

Shells derived particular interest in the South Seas because their use as ornaments was often regulated by rigid sumptuary laws confining them to particular grades in society. As a man's shell ornaments denoted his status in society, if you were able to kill him and seize them, all his personal prestige would accrue to yourself — for as long as you could keep them, that is. So shell ornaments became a badge of personal prowess. Among some tribes of the Admiralty Islands the round shell pendants called *kap kaps* could only be worn by someone who had killed his man in battle. The Friendly Island chieftains wore a scarce orange cowrie as a badge of their office. Only a few cone shells could be found on the Solomons large enough to make the armlets which were the most highly prized treasure of the South Seas, so prized that wars were often fought for the possession of a single armlet, by comparison with

which human life was looked on as utterly worthless. Great chiefs and warriors made a point of wearing several of these bangles on their arms, knowing full well that (like the medals Nelson insisted on wearing at Trafalgar) they were a distinction which would make them the target for every missile in the battle, while in peacetime they were liable to be knocked on the head just for the sake of their ornaments.

Women had their shell ornaments too, but they were usually less elaborate than those worn by the vain sex. Necklaces were given to girls as betrothal presents, but *kap kaps* were felt to be so special that they could only be lent for a short while to girls going through the painful ordeal of initiation, so as to keep their spirits up. Once the wounds of the initiates had healed they had to return the *kap kaps* to the male relatives who had lent them.

The nature of Oceanic society contributed to the development of shell carving. The concept of the taboo, by which certain articles were thought to be appropriate only for chiefs, meant that these royal objects would be continually produced and offered

Maori chiefs' storehouses with human figure posts with inlaid eyes of shell. From J. G. Wood, Natural History of Man *(London: 1875), p. 49. Photograph courtesy Stella Mayes Reed.*

as tribute or gifts. The inlaid wood and mother-of-pearl bowls in which sweet wine was served to distinguished guests by chiefs in the Pelew Islands is a case in point. The caste structure of New Zealand society enabled corps of specialists to develop at more than one level. The Maori aristocrat, or *rangatira,* had no occupation save war. He was so aristocratic that it was taboo for him to do any menial work, so much so that if he had no slave to carry his food for him on a journey he would simply have to starve. Apart from hunting, there was only one peacetime occupation open to the *rangatira* — art. "He may perhaps," say Wood, "condescend to carve the posts of his house into some fantastical semblance of the human form." House posts bore the shell eyes which were one of the principal items in Maori shell carving; so too did another Maori *chef d'oeuvre* which apparently was made by no one

save chiefs — the boxes which contained the most prized adornment of the Maori, the tail feathers of the *neomorpha gouldii.* The beautiful black-and-white tail plumes of this species of hoopoe were worn by high-ranking chiefs as an ear ornament. The feather boxes were usually covered with a design of interlocking animals or birds, whose eyes were picked out in abalone shell. Maoris of chiefly rank would also carve the figures known as *tikis* which, like the carvings of ancient America, were a composite of jade and shell.

Another artistic class were the priests or *tohungas,* who were the recipients of the folklore and religion of the Maoris, much of which entered into their carvings. A further class of art workers were the slaves, who might be given specialist duties, such as tattooing. Slaves had to work, unlike chiefs or priests, so their output was continuous. No one was ever pressed to finish a job in old New Zealand, however. A chief did not care whether the grass mat which was being woven for him took six months, or four years, to finish, and the craftworker did not care either. What mattered was that the mat should be beautifully made, exact in finish and original in design, so that when the chief put it on he would stand out from his fellows. The strongly individualistic nature of Maori society which encouraged any *rangatira* who was sufficiently brave and popular to become a chief, also provided local centers of patronage, in which craftsmen would be urged to produce ornaments more attractive than those in the next *pah,* or fortress village.

In order to cater for the tastes of the highly placed clientele who were their principal patrons, the islanders had patiently acquired simple but extremely effective techniques of craftsmanship. Even the Tasmanians, earth's most primitive inhabitants, had noticed that *elenchus irisodonta* shells acquired a brilliant iridescence once they had been cast on the shore and the cuticle had become decomposed. They found that they could put the shells through the same process artifically by exposing them to a thick, dense smoke from burning greenery. This bonfire gave off pyroligneous acid, which ate away the cuticle of the shell. The Tasmanians also employed an alternative method; they rubbed the shells with vinegar obtained from the English settlers to remove the epidermis, and boiled them with tea to heighten their characteristic blue and green tint before rubbing them with fat to polish them. Once polished, the Tasmanians drilled the shell beads by nipping them between their teeth. When strung on kangaroo sinews, the shell necklaces looked so attractive that soon English ladies began to demand similar ones.

In New Zealand, abalone shell was worked to a

Oceanic headdress of tortoiseshell and pearl shell.
Courtesy British Museum, London.

Kap kaps worn as a headband, Marquesas Islands. Courtesy British Museum, London.

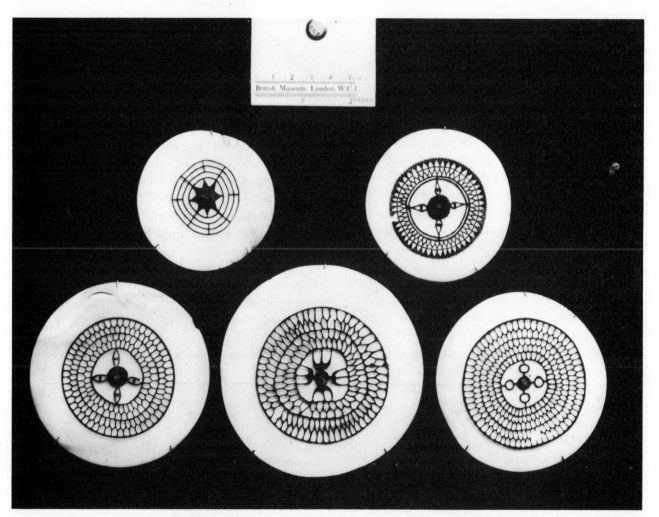

A Western artist equipped with the most advanced tools would find it hard to carve these almost incredibly delicate patterns. Oceanic kap kaps. Courtesy British Museum, London.

Kap kaps (tortoiseshell inlays on tridacna shell) from the Admiralty Islands. Courtesy British Museum, London.

high polish with a rubbing stone and sand. In Melanesia the enormous shell of the Giant Clam was cut into sections with saws made from sharpened bivalve shells, and trimmed down with adzes, also made from *tridacna*. Notched saws were used as scrapers to smooth the surface of the kap kap mounts, which were finally polished to a surface resembling white marble or alabaster by grinding the shell on a stone with sand and water. The holes by which kap kaps were suspended around the neck were drilled with a simple bow drill, using a point made from the sharp end of a *terebra* or *mitra* shell. For boring rings in the *tridacna,* drills made from bamboo, coral, or pumice stone were used.

In order to work tortoise shell, it was first softened by heating it in hot water, or by placing it directly on hot coals. The shell was cut by means of a saw consisting of a string of twisted bamboo epidermis, and drilled with a rotating drill made from a shark's tooth. In the Huon Gulf area of New Guinea, the tortoiseshell ornaments worn were particularly fine. Selected pieces of shell taken from hawksbill and green turtles which had been caught accidentally in the nets were sorted out according to the type of ornament which was to be made from them. Pieces for bracelets were selected from the side of the carapace. These were straightened out by heat; the outside was ground with sand and pieces of obsidian, the inside sanded. Next the plates of tortoiseshell were polished with a piece of wood, and then cut into wide plaques by means

of a wooden straight edge. The design for the pattern was also inscribed with a straight edge, while a kap kap was used as a compass.

The designs used by the South Sea shell carver were traditional, and there was much overlapping between shell carving and other arts. Tattoo patterns might appear in wood carving. Geometric designs were extremely popular over the greater part of the area. Birds and animals were also used, sometimes in a very simplified form, other times in an extremely elaborated one. In its most distorted form an animal or human figure might be related to very esoteric concepts from the island's mythology, such as "sea ghosts", stylized double-headed snakes, twin eyes, ancestor figures, or those of cult heroes. Many of the best designs, such as those on the kap kaps, were purely abstract.

Shell ornaments were extremely varied, but not all of them merit exhaustive discussion from the artistic point of view. The kap kap, which has already been mentioned several times, was a round pendant, sometimes ornamented with tortoiseshell overlay or engraved, which was in use almost universally over the South Seas, even in distant Australia. It was extremely similar to the shell pendant worn by the Indians of the northern states and called a *runtee*. It is much more difficult to make a perfectly round shell ornament than one in any other shape, so it is all the more striking that peoples so far apart should have worn similar pendants, just as is the use of shell money, on both sides of the Pacific.

In its most attractive form a kap kap was a mount of white shell upon which a thin ornament of fretted tortoiseshell had been placed. The two were fastened together by a knotted string drawn through a hole in the center. Methods of wearing

Kap kap worn as a headband, Oceania. Courtesy British Museum (Ethnography), London.

Melanesian pearl shell and tridacna shell pendants.
Courtesy Anthropological Museum of Aberdeen University.

*Melanesian pearl shell pendants. Courtesy Anthro-
pological Museum of Aberdeen University.*

Maori Tiki with inlaid shell eyes and nipples. New Zealand. Courtesy British Museum, London.

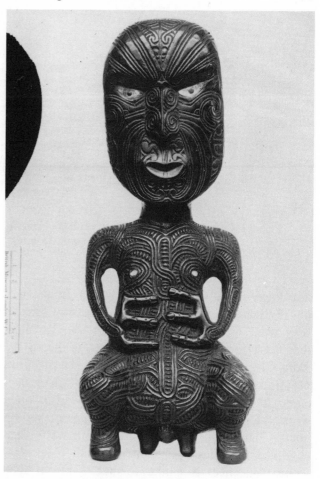

CARVED FEATHER-BOXES.

Maori-carved feather boxes, showing inlaid eyes. From J. G. Wood, Natural History of Man *(London: 1875), p. 127. Photograph courtesy Stella Mayes Reed.*

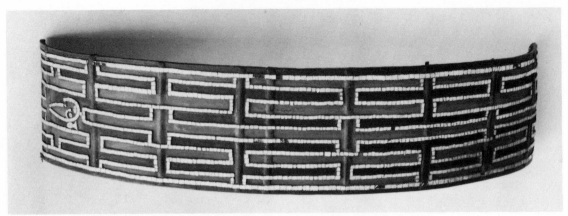

Solomon Islands shield, inlaid with shell. Courtesy British Museum, London.

kap kaps varied from island to island. In the Admiralty Islands, where some of the best were made, they were worn as ring chains. In the Carolines they took the form of ear pendants, while in the Admiralty Islands they hung round the neck as pectorals. The ornament on the smaller tortoiseshell circle in the center of the kap kap was in open work, often in designs which were also employed on gourds. The plain, round shell pendants were often engraved with designs heightened with black pigment. The effect is similar to that of mixed shell and tortoiseshell. Pendants from the Solomon Islands are representative of the best work of this sort. In addition to the round pendants there are many of drop shape, like the *dibbi dibbi* of Australia. Closely related to kap kap are the headbands worn in Marquesas. These might embody either one large shell and tortoiseshell circlet in kap kap style or several small ones.

Tortoiseshell was fished throughout all the islands, and some, such as the Marquesas, were regularly visited by white traders who came to collect the shell. The local fishermen would swim or paddle out to the trading schooner and haggle over each individual plate of shell, instead of trying to sell the whole "head," or carapace, at once. So they had every chance to select the best piece of shell for a particular piece of art work.

In New Guinea, beautiful cylinder-shaped bangles were made in the Sepik area. Throughout the island very intricate bracelets and earrings were engraved by means of a boar's tooth fixed in a wooden handle. Simple dogtooth, lizard, snail-bead, eye, and ribbon

motifs were elaborated into the most complex and satisfying patterns. Superb tortoiseshell bracelets of this sort were reserved for males at festival times. Only young men could wear earrings, because the taboo forced married men in mourning to slit their ears. Tortoiseshell pendants could also be worn around the neck. Ornaments were also clenched between the teeth when fighting or dancing because it was thought that an open mouth was an ugly sight, which was just the opposite belief to that held in New Zealand, where a thrust-out tongue was considered to be the supreme manifestation of warlike defiance.

In the Torres Straits, tortoiseshell was used for figures and headdresses. The most ambitious shell carvings made in the South Seas were also constructed there. These were the tortoiseshell masks, in which the largest available back plates, stitched together, were used. The extremities of the mask and the nose were molded separately and attached subsequently. Design was worked onto the mask, usually in the form of a few simple motifs, and eyes and mouth were filled with shell insets and touched up with appropriately colored paints.

Enough has been said to indicate the extrordinary diversity of shell ornaments in the South Seas. There was no part of the body, from the septum of the nose, through which were thrust antlerlike spreading ornaments, to the glans of the penis, which was covered with an engraved shell, that did not receive its appropriate decoration.

In addition to ornaments, wampum, which is virtually identical with that made in North Amer-

Mask in tortoiseshell from Torres Straits, New Guinea,
surrounded by an open work frieze now partly broken.

Wooden model of a dog inlaid with pearl shell. Solomon Islands. Courtesy British Museum, London.

Wooden bowl inlaid with pearl shell from San Cristoval, Solomon Islands. Courtesy British Museum, London.

Stone-headed club haft inlaid with pearl shell from the Solomon Islands. Courtesy British Museum (Ethnography), London.

ica, is recorded from the Oleai, in the Caroline Islands. like very early Red Indian wampum, it was made with white shell beads interspersed with black wooden ones — pieces of black coconut shell

If the existence of wampum on both sides of the Pacific argues that some measure of diffusion took place, and that shell carving moved from continent to continent, so too does shell inlay, which stretches, literally, from China to Peru. Even more striking than the mere existence of shell inlay in America and Asia at the same time is the fact that on the islands of the Pacific the carver made use of standard prefabricated pieces of shell, which could be fitted into virtually any type of design, just as the Aztec artist did.

The uses of inlay in the South Seas were very extended. They included the decoration of canoes, statues, house gables, models, clubs, masks, fishing floats, bowls, and many other objects. Whenever South Sea inlay appears it is immediately recognizable because of its unique qualities of verve and originality, though the inlay of Polynesia, in Manihiki for example, does resemble somewhat that used on the Asiatic mainland.

The most familiar type of Pacific shell inlay is perhaps that used by the Maoris. Eyes of abalone shell appear in carved heads, boxes for feathers, and *tikis,* as well as on the giant statue pillars which held up the roofs of the houses or figured as ridgepole ornaments.

The high place held by shell carving in Maori art can be conceived from a description of the tomb which Te Whero erected for his favorite daughter in the middle of his great *pah* of Raroera. Before its destruction, it was sketched by Angas and described by Wood. The whole of the tomb was covered with human heads, of which there were fourteen on the front alone, exclusive of the pillars, each of which consisted of two human figures standing one on the head of the other. "Their enormous eyes," wrote Wood, "are made peculiarly conspicuous by being carved out of haliotis shell." In fact the face, with staring shell eyes, was the point in New Zealand architecture to which the eye of the specator was particularly directed. In the most famous of all Maori buildings, the war house of the ruthless cannibal chief Rangihaeta, all the enemy warriors, whom the chief had first slain and then

Vessels with pearl shell inlay. Note design on right showing warriors carrying severed heads. Courtesy British Museum, London.

Container with pearl shell inlay, Oceania. British Museum, London.

Prow of a canoe, inlaid with shell, from the Solomon Islands. Courtesy British Museum (Ethnography), London.

devoured, and his own warriors were represented, the latter with their tongues thrust out in defiance. The figure at the end of the ridgepole, over the door, represented the owner of the house, and was given particular attention.

The use of multiple shell inlays reached its height in the Solomon Islands. There a large canoe might carry as many as five rows of pearl shell inlay on each side of its stem and stern posts, and more along the side of the canoe. A row might contain as many as 99 shell inlay plaques, counting just from the top of the stem down to the waterline. The islanders had perfected the use of prepared shapes made in just a few standard forms. There were many advantages in the use of such components; because they were all the same size (apart from

custom-built pieces made to solve some particular artistic problem) they looked very effective when massed in groups or arranged in lines. The regularity of their size no doubt related to the shapes which could be made most conveniently from the average shell available—larger pieces of shell were kept for the special shapes which I mentioned above. Moreover the carver could specialize in making a particular shape over and over again, thus both increasing his skill and cutting the time required to do the job. He might even develop special tools, such as *tridacna* saws shaped to cut just one type of nick in a serrated wheel. What was more, he did not have to be continually leaving his carvings to design new shapes and could keep up his output—no small consideration in view of

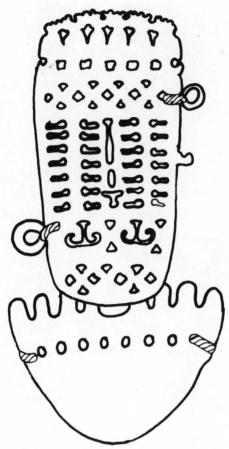

Ceremonial standard made from pieces of tridacna shell lashed together and carried in the bows of head-hunting canoes in the Solomons.

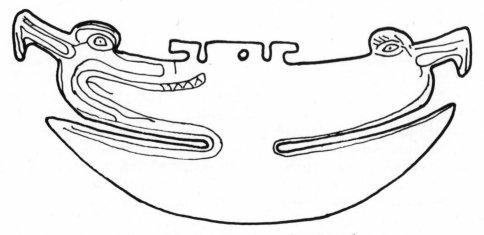

Solomon Islands pendant in mother-of-pearl.

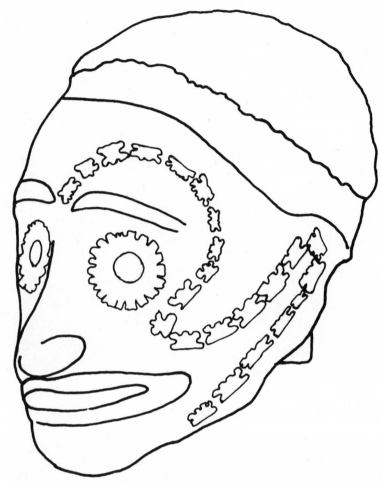

Head modeled over a skull and inset with mother-of-pearl "prefabricated" shapes. Solomon Islands.

the numbers of components required. No doubt many shell carvers were at work furnishing plaques for just one canoe—which must have seemed a floating treasure house to the men who sailed in her. Shell carving was a laborious task, however, and even the smallest piece of ornament must have been regarded as a treasure, coveted by others, and the prized possession of whoever owned it.

Although incredibly diversified, the repertoire of South Sea shell carving did not include the cameo, one reason for its absence being that the islanders never possessed the steel chisels necessary to sculpt the hard exterior of a shell. The cameoed pearl shells from New Caledonia which are represented in at least two collections in Britain are the work of Frenchmen, to judge from the inscriptions which they carry. The number of honest Frenchmen in

New Caledonia was far outweighed by those who had left their country for their country's good. In 1864 New Caledonia became a penal colony of France; in 1898 it ceased to admit new prisoners; but as late as 1901 there was still a convict population of more than 10,000.

A high proportion of these prisoners was the remnant of the Communards. Between 18th March and 28th May, 1871, the Parisians had set up a separate government, as opposed to the National Assembly of Versailles. The revolt was a protest against the crushing terms of the surrender of France to Germany after the Franco-Prussian war and specific grievances, such as the demand for rent due during the siege of Paris and the disarming of the National Guard. Although originally just a collection of patriotic Frenchmen with vague views on

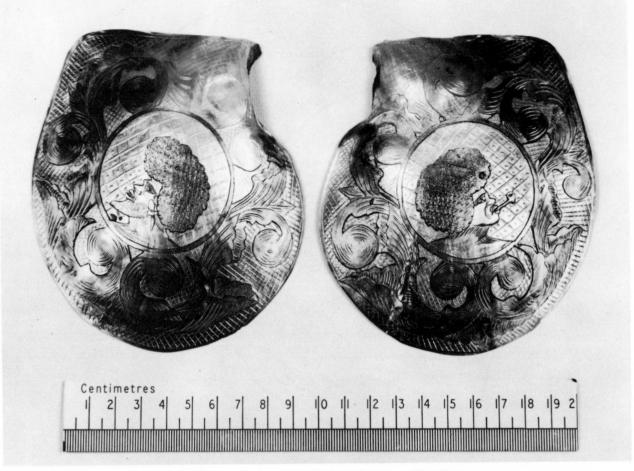

Carved pearl shells from New Caledonia. The European ornament which enters into these shells (diaper and leaf designs) and the rude style of caricature in which the figures are drawn, shows that they were carved by the white and not the black inhabitants of New Caledonia, and they are probably the work of French convicts.

socialist federalism, under the stress of attack from without by the hated provincials and manipulation from within by bands of extremists, the Commune soon became a terror machine, forcing uncommitted French civilians, and even American and English tourists who had been trapped in Paris when the second siege began, to don the Communard uniform and man the walls. When the collapse of the beleaguered city came, the Communards demonstrated that there was no trick to savagery, achieving a state of barbarism considerably lower than that of the South Sea islanders by massacring hostages and burning down some of the loveliest buildings in Paris, including the Louvre. Not surprisingly, reprisals by the Versailles Assembly were harsh. Thousands of Communards were sent to New Caledonia. As they were Parisians, they may have included men from the jewelry trades, perhaps even cameists. Nine years after the Commune there were not fewer than 3,000 cameo cutters in the French capital, to which the art had been introduced in 1853.

Forceful, crude, yet interesting and impressive, these shells represent an art genre which was unappreciated, because unknown, before I discovered one series in an aquarium, one in an anthropologi-

Another similar shell. The legend reads, "La Chasse aux Nouveau Caledoniens" (New Caledonians Hunting). Courtesy Manchester Museum, England.

*Nineteenth-century carved pearl shell from New Cale-
donia. Manchester Museum, England.*

cal museum, in provincial centers in Britain far from the normal beat of art historians. These masterpieces of prisoners' work unite in their composition the two principal colors of Pacific shell carving, pearl and gold, although in their case the gold is not that of tortoiseshell carving but of dark gold-colored conchyolin which, on the outside of the shell covers the pearly sheen of nacre. They form a sad postscript to a chapter of art which has now closed for ever.

6

Scallop of Salvation:
Mother-of-Pearl in the Near East

MOTHER-OF-PEARL IS THE TERM APPLIED TO THE iridescent lining of a group of shells which yield pearls. Mother-of-pearl is made of exactly the same substance as a pearl. The only feature of pearls which differs from the base or matrix from which they sprang is their extreme rarity. Pearl is so akin to the lining of the pearl shell that it is not unknown for pearls which have formed to become assimilated to the lining once more, so that they have to be cut out from it. The American buccaneer, Dampier, pointed out long ago that mother-of-pearl is more shining and resplendent than pearls themselves. The group of shells which produces mother-of-pearl, or "mop" as it is called affectionately by people who trade in it, is so numerous that it would be tedious to mention them all. They include the ordinary nautilus, the paper nautilus, the *turbo* shells, the *trochas,* the gaint snail, and a wide variety of mussels. None of these shells produces mother-of-pearl in such large or workable quantities as the great pearl oyster or *meleagrina margaritifera,* however, which for practical purposes is the source of most of the mother-of-pearl to be discussed in this and the subsequent chapter.

Before describing how pearl oysters are fished, it may be useful to describe the substance of mother-of-pearl, or nacre, as it is sometimes called. Like every other kind of shell material, mother-of-pearl is deposited on the inside of the shell by the mantle which encircles the body of the mollusk. It is laid down on the inside surface in silvery shining parallel folds. Nacre is aragonite, a mineral also found on land. Nacre, however, is iridescent, whereas terrestial aragonite is not, because the calcium carbonate which composes the mother-of-pearl has been laid down in gently undulating waves or ridges. The great Scottish scientist, Sir David Brewster, first pointed out that the pearly lustre and iridescence of nacre arose from the fact that we find in all mother-of-pearl "a grooved structure upon its surface, resembling very closely the delicate texture of the skin at the top of an infant's finger, or the minute corrugations which are often seen on surfaces covered with varnish or with oil paint." By imitating the corrugated substance of nacre, scientists found that they could transfer the phenomenon of iridiscence to other substances, such as wax or steel. Nacre does not compose the whole of the inside of the pearl oyster. Its exterior is formed of a hard, horny, brown substance called *conchyolin.* This contains much more organic material than does nacre, as can be seen from the smell it produces while it is being ground off.

Mother-of-pearl can be sawed into slabs, and ground, without destroying the iridescence of the material. Each new surface shows a corrugated exterior capable of reflecting light lustrously. It is possible for the surface of nacre, however to become "blind," that is, lose its iridescence. Shell merchants attribute this change to great exposure to the sun.

No art material, not even ivory from the forests of the Congo or gems from the deepest mine, has ever been acquired with greater difficulty or danger than mother-of-pearl. The fact that every particle of it has been brought to the surface at the peril of the diver's life shows how desired this material has always been. The method of fishing for pearls on the Malabar coast will serve as a description for most pearl fisheries. The fishing was only carried on for six weeks in the year, beginning in February, and ending about the beginning of April. The divers traveled to the fishing grounds (which were

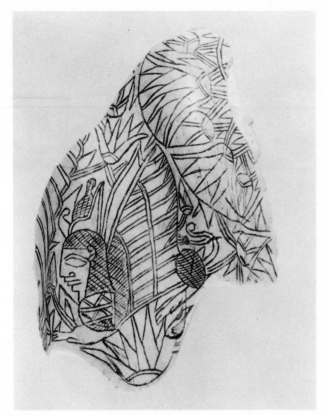

Fragment of engraved shell from Kuyunjik (Nineveh) about 7th century B.C. Courtesy British Museum, London.

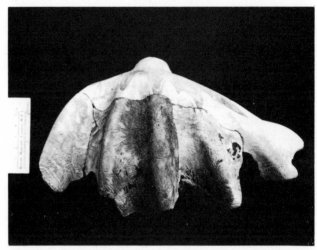

Carved tridacna shell from Babylonia, seventh century B.C. Courtesy British Museum, London.

When it happens, it is useless to hope to make anything from the shell, unless it can be split. The scientific reasons for the "blindness," are discussed elsewhere.

There are many variations in the types of *meleagrinas* which produce nacre. These shells are fished, not for their mother-of-pearl, but for the pearls they contain. An exception to this rule are those fisheries which supply the China trade. Mother-of-pearl has been a profitable import to China at least since the days of the Persian Empire. Shell from the Persian Gulf was distributed through Europe, via Danzig, for use in carving and inlay work. The Japanese and Chinese carvers drew their supplies from the Dutch East Indies. The best shell nowadays comes from Australian waters. It is white, as opposed to the "golden lip," an amber-colored shell which is characteristic of the Philippines. From Tahiti and the Cook Islands comes the famous "black lip," a dark, smoky-colored shell.

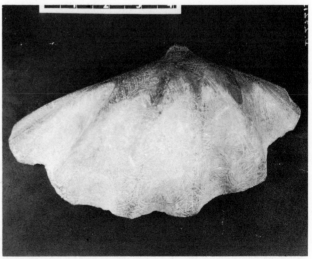

Engraved tridacna shell from near Bethlehem. Courtesy British Museum, London.

about six or seven hours' sail from the coast) in large boats which sailed in convoy, at a signal from the starting gun. Each boat carried about twenty men, with a *tindal,* or chief boatman, as pilot. Ten of the crew were rowers; they also hauled up the sink stones of the divers, and the other ten collected the pearls from the bottom. The divers had been swimming from infancy; they could descend to the bottom in up to ten fathoms of water, and stay for up to two minutes. A section of five divers went overboard at one time, leaving the other five to rest. When the time came to drop overboard, the diver seized a triangular sink stone of red granite, attached to a rope, with the toes of his right foot, gripped a network bag in his left, and, holding his nostrils with his left hand, sank to the bottom. He held a haul rope in his right hand. As soon as he reached the bottom and filled his net with oysters, he would give the signal to be pulled up. As he surfaced, he would bear witness of the strain to which he had been subjected. His ears and nostrils would frequently be bleeding, his body covered with the sores acquired from rubbing against the bottom. Occasionally, as he surfaced with a rich haul of oysters, his heart would give out and he would die in the arms of his shipmates as they drew him aboard. The British poet Procter seized on this incident in a poem:

> Within the midnight of her hair,
> Half hidden in its deepest deeps
> A single, peerless, priceless pearl
> All filmy-eyed for ever sleeps
> He who plucked it from its bed
> In the far blue Indian Ocean
> Lieth, without life or motion
> In his earthy dwelling, dead.
> And his children one by one
> When they look upon the sun,
> Curse the toil by which he drew
> The treasure from its bed of blue.

The motive which induced pearl fishers to spend, or rather squander, their lives on this dangerous, irksome, and unrewarding trade was the hope that one day they would find a pearl so magnificent that they could live on it in comfort for the rest of their lives. Sometimes they were allotted a share of the oysters, sometimes they were allowed all the pearls they caught, but most often they simply stole and successfully secreted the pearls which they had noticed in the oysters as they gaped in the heat of

Pillar from the temple at Al-Ubaid in southern Iraq, about 2500 B.C. The designs used are virtually identical with the inlay, in similar shell, which appears on Egyptian musical instruments of the nineteenth century. British Museum, London.

the sun, and snatched out.

The arrival of the diving suit merely added to the dangers of the diver, especially on the coast of California, where many of the richest pearls were to be found. Lieutenant Hardy, an English naval officer, went to California in 1825 to reorganize the pearl fishery, which had in early colonial times been carried on by slave divers who were treated with great cruelty by their Spanish masters. It was now in the hands of free divers such as Pablo Ochon, who dived after pearls with no other weapon than a short, pointed stick to fight off the *tintereros* (ground sharks capable of swallowing a diver whole) and manta rays. Pablo had escaped from one particularly desperate encounter with a *tinterero* by stirring up a cloud of sand from the bottom of the sea and surfacing under cover of this improvised smoke screen. In an attempt to revital-

Shell plaques from Ur, dated about 2500 B.C. They were originally used to inlay mosaics like the Royal Standard. Courtesy British Museum, London.

ize the fishery, Hardy taught himself how to dive, using a diving dress. He found he could only get down two or three fathoms, "at which depth the pressure of the water on the ears is so great that I can only compare it to a sharp-pointed iron instrument being violently forced into that organ." He had been assured by other divers that as soon as his eardrums had burst he would be able to dive deeper. In order to hasten this process, he dropped to seven fathoms, when, "I felt a sensation in my ears like that produced by the explosion of a gun." Even in a suit, Hardy found the diver pitiably exposed, not merely to the danger of the "bends,"—decompression sickness—but to the creatures of the deep. "Every fathom," he wrote, "fills the imagination with some new idea of the dangerous folly of penetrating farther into the silent dominions of reckless monsters, where the skulls of the dead make perpetual grimaces, and the yawning jaws of sharks and tintereros, or the death-embrace of the manta, lie in wait for us."

Just as dangers have never deterred the diver, so the difficulties of shell carving have never prevented the craftsman from employing nacre, one of the most rewarding of all materials. In the Middle East, the story of pearl shell carving forms a unique chapter in the history of art. It dawns, in the earliest prehistory, reaches a peak at the time of Ur of the Chaldees, about two and a half thousand years before Christ, recedes somewhat, and then returns with much of its original vigor to constitute the most

forceful school of today. "The mother-of-pearl encrusted furniture with which the bazaars of Damascus are stocked today is the degenerate but direct descendant of an applied art brought to the its highest pitch by the Sumerians of the fourth millenium B.C.," wrote Leonard Woolley, after an American-financed expedition had laid bare the riches of royal Ur. History has revised his dating, but not his dictum. It is only necessary to add that shell carving is an art which has always had the closest associations with religion, from the time when Sumerian worshippers bowed before an image of shell mosaic down to our own day, when the pilgrim to the Holy Land brings back with him a nacre memento of the shrines of Jerusalem and Bethlehem.

The early Neolithic inhabitants of Palestine and Jordan employed the *dentalium* shell, shaped

Sumerian mosaic inlay plaque. Courtesy British Museum, London.

Side view of the Standard of Ur. The constrained positions of the men and animal figures have been caused by mistakes made in recovering the mosaic tesserae from their original, scattered position. Dated about 2500 B.C. Courtesy British Museum, London.

craftsmen labored in cubicles a meter wide and two meters long. Piled up on their workroom floors were cowries and mother-of-pearl from the Red Sea. Already shell was associated with other precious materials with which it would have a long run in harness, materials such as malachite, which would be combined with nacre by sculptors of the English Decorative School. After work the carvers relaxed on a comfortable dais in front of a circular hearth fire, in spacious living quarters ornamented with fine lime-plaster walls painted in red and cream.

By the time of the flowering of the civilization of Ur, in the third millenium B.C., all the best-known forms of shell decoration had been invented. They included shell carving in relief; shell inlay, in which shell was combined with other precious materials to form a mosaic; shell engraving, in which shell plaques were incised with designs; and even a form of shell intarsia, which is not heard of after Ur, in which the surface of the shell was hollowed out and then filled with colored composition.

Shell had probably come into use in Ur because it was a substitute for limestone. The sculptors of Ur had already evolved a technique in which silhouette figures modeled in low relief were sculpted from limestone and sunk into a bed of bitumen. A well-known frieze of this sort, dating from the first half of the third millenium, decorated the temple

like a hollow elephant tusk, which could be easily pierced and strung. Beads made in this way were arranged in diadems or caps, and some of the finest buried with the dead. In addition to their use as ornaments, shells became interesting to craftsmen of the Holy Land for their supposed amuletic value. In Jericho, finely modeled plaster heads were molded around skulls (presumably of revered ancestors) and cowries with staringly contrasting spots, like pupils, were inserted to serve as eyes. By the seventh millenium B.C., shell carving had evolved as a specialist art. At Beidha, an important center for trade routes from the desert to the Mediterranean coast, and from the Red Sea to the Jordan valley, a complete bazaar of workshops arranged around living quarters was unearthed. The

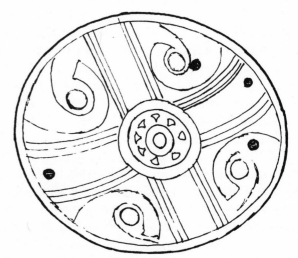

Half of a pair of shell clappers from ancient Nimrud. The perforations originally held rivets to attach the clapper to a handle.

of Al 'Ubaid. Limestone figures appear side by side with shell ones on the "Royal Standard" of Ur. In the process of conversion from limestone to shell, the high-modeled figures made in limestone have become flattened because shell is a hard and brittle material. Another factor which produced the rise of shell carving is this very hardness. Shell would not wear away, as would limestone, and it might lend a resonant tone to the musical instruments which were decorated with it—such as the famous lyres. Most of the materials which go to decorate musical instruments, at one period of history or another, are considered to have a beneficial effect on their tone, and it is noticeable that mother-of-pearl is still widely used for inlay on musical instruments, on those made in Spain and the Middle East for example. Pearl shell inlay had been feeling its way into Sumerian art for some time, begin-

ning with quite small decorative objects, such as the stone bowl ornamented with nacre inlay set in bitumen found in the temple of Khafajah and dated from 3000 B.C. Almost certainly shell inlay on stone had been preceded by similar inlay on a core of wood. The columns of the Pillar Temple at Uruk, which are decorated with triangles and diamond-shaped pieces of mother-of-pearl, in alternate bands, date only from about 2,600 B.C., but there may be earlier examples. The decoration of these pillars is a striking commentary on the continuity of shell carving in Eastern lands. The same ornamentation elements, once more arranged in alternate bands, appear on a *darabouka* from Egypt, made in the nineteenth century.

From the probable beginnings of shell mosaic in Mesopotamia, which were confined to purely geometrical patterns of inlay, figure subjects begin to

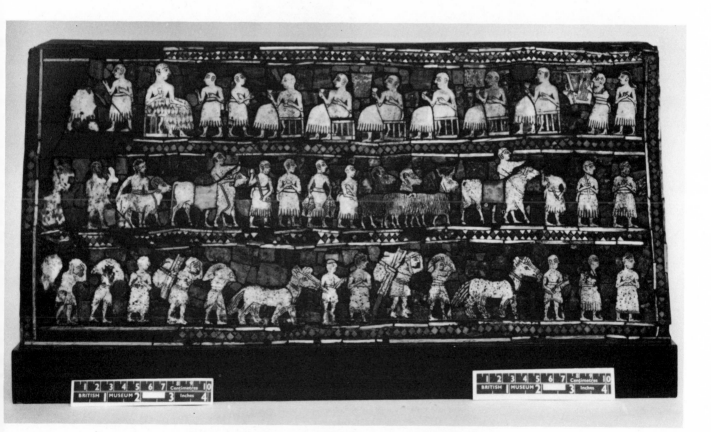

Part of the famous Standard of Ur, of 2500 B.C. Perhaps the most important piece of Sumerian sculpture, it may be the sounding box of a lyre or harp, and is inlaid with shell, red limestone, and lapis lazuli, inlaid in bitumen. The Aztecs of Mexico set their mosaics in a similar groundwork. Courtesy British Museum, London.

The Ram Caught in a Thicket. Probably the most famous of all Sumerian sculptures, this figure is now generally accepted to be a he-goat. The horns, beard, and locks of hair are carved in shell or lapis lazuli. From Ur, dated around 2500 B.C. Courtesy British Museum, London.

emerge, as on the fragmentary "Standard of Mari," made in the first half of the third millenium B.C. For the first time we have style, and the possibility of at least guessing what techniques were used. The "Standard," which was probably the sounding box for a lyre, shows dignitaries walking in procession, worshippers sacrificing, and a seated figure drinking from a cup. The use of the drill, which has been used to form the eyes of the figures, is already evident. The zigzag lines of some of the more unskillful carvers of the team which produced the standard show that they must have been using a straight-edged tool, such as a burin or chisel. With a tool such as this it is easier to begin a curved line and turn it into two straight ones than with a pointed style. The raw material for shell carving at this time included the large conch shells found in the Persian Gulf, as well as pearl shell. Flat plaques could be cut from the conch shells, small in size but suitable for inlay. They have been described as having "the color and grain of ivory, and a surface no less smooth and fine." This is certainly not true of any examples I have seen.

It is worth emphasizing that conch would be much harder, and much more brittle, than nacre. Another Mari technique which is worth mentioning is the deep engraving of lines which are afterwards filled with bitumen. This and other techniques were employed with triumphant success on the objects found in the Royal Grave of Ur (2,500 B.C.), They include gaming boards, sounding boxes for harps, inlaid shell lamps, and other mosaic objects.

Gaming board and playing pieces from the Royal Grave of Ur, about 2500 B.C. This game, which was probably the possession of the King of Ur, was made from a wooden board inlaid with colored paste, lapis lazuli (from Afghanistan), and shell. "Every square," wrote its discoverer, Sir Leonard Woolley, "must have its own pattern and every tessera rank as a gem." Courtesy British Museum, London.

The most famous find was the "Royal Standard," an oblong sounding box with sides about eighteen inches long. Its side profiles have the shape of a truncated obelisk. On the back and front of the box are scenes from daily life, with war on one side and peace on the other, while the ends deal with the unseen universe. They are concerned with mythological scenes in which men mingle with the gods.

Shell is handled much more skillfully here than it was at Mari. The artist has given up the difficult task of cutting the hard material into a modeled relief. Instead he contents himself with a flat, scrimshaw technique, in which the engraved lines are filled in with substantial black inlay. He is now able to manipulate much smaller pieces of inlay, in a style which is moving towards *pietra dura* work. The old architectural inlays of diamonds and triangles resurrect themselves in these mosaics. In the gaming board, scrimshaw designs are applied to the tesserae to give an impression of imitation inlay.

A little more information is now available concerning technique. Tesserae which the Department of Western Antiquities in the British Museum kindly allowed me to examine with a 25 X magnifying glass showed no evidence of the use of a saw. This is hardly surprising as there is no record of

saws having been used at this early date. They did however bear plain marks of having been shaped with a rubbing stone. Under the magnifying glass, tiny parallel groove lines could be seen on the surface. These ran fairly straight, but with an occasional change in direction. Evidently the pieces of shell had been broken into suitable fragments and then rubbed down to the correct shape with a block of sandstone, or some similar stone. Alternatively they might have been cut by a cord coated with abrasive. Once again there was evidence of a straight-sided graver.

Great skill was required to form the engraved tesserae and plaques, and considerable care was necessary to carve the whole tridacna shells represented by several finds from the time of Ur. This is, as has been said, a hard and brittle shell. Shells of this sort, engraved all over, carry over from Sumerian times to a much more recent period. One was found at Camina in Etruria. It dates from the sixth or seventh century before Christ and is probably of Phoenician workmanship.

Shell carving, which had developed rather mysteriously around 3000 B.C., and which had flourished between 2,750 and 2450 B.C., now disappears, for reasons which are not apparent. For

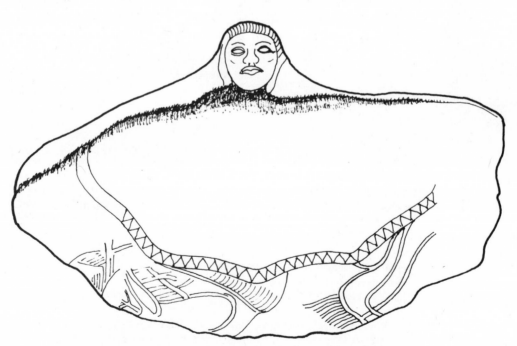

Carced tridacna *shell found in Etruria but probably of Phoenician workmanship. Sixth or seventh century B.C.*

Box of wood inlaid with mother-of-pearl from Gujerat, India, sixteenth or seventeenth century. Courtesy Victoria and Albert Museum, London.

the succeeding ages in Mesopotamian history (from the sixteenth century B.C. onwards) the favored material for inlay is not shell, but ivory. Between the disappearance of pearl shell carving in one grave—the Royal Tomb of Ur—in 2,500 B.C. and its reappearance outside another—the Church of the Holy Sepulchre—in the late Middle Ages, its history is conjecture.

To the Muslim Arabs who conquered most of the East from the sixth century A.D. onwards, it was an unholy thing to carve the image of any lving creature. An artist who attempted this would, on the Last Day, be ordered by Allah to give life to his creation, and be destroyed when he failed to do so. This belief, which was not basic to Islam but was

introduced by Jewish converts to the faith, put an end to figure designs, such as those which have been just been described, in all Muslim countries. Pearl shell carving, however, continued to flourish in the form of geometrical and abstract design. The main center for its employment passed from Mesopotamia to Persia, where it flourished in the shape of intarsia—a combination inlay of many different materials in furniture. From Persia, it moved to Mohammedan India. In 1424 Ahmad Shah, a Muslim Indian conqueror, converted the Hindu temple at Amedabad into the Jama Masjid mosque, one of the most famous buildings in India. Let into the marble tomb of one of his queens was elaborate mother-of-pearl inlay. Ahmedabad became an im-

portant center for mother-of-pearl craftsmen, who
fashioned the intarsia work on the wooden canopies
over the shrines of Shah Alam at Sarkhej. When the
world at large began to take a belated interest in
the arts of India, mother-of-pearl work had died out
in Ahmedabad. An inquirer into the art in 1879,
however, learned that the simpler pieces of intarsia
had been formed by filing pieces of nacre to the
required size and letting them into a pattern cut
into the wood. The more elaborate designs had
been made up by laying fragments of differently
colored shell, set in cement, onto the surface to be
ornamented. By 1879, only a small amount of
coarse inlay was being made. And so often happens
with shell inlay, it was applied to the frames and
finger boards of instruments, in this case *tambura*
and *rubabs*.

As soon as pearl inlay passed out of a Muslim
into a non-Muslim country, its confinement to geometrical and abstracts shapes was forgotten, and
human figures appear once more. The revival of
the human and animal form in inlay is particularly
striking in Siam. Unlike the Indians, the Siamese
maintained their craft traditions, helped by the
judicious patronage of the King of Siam, who was
Anna Leonowens employer—King Mongkut. The
King, who was deeply anxious that Siam should
resume the progress it had abandoned in the Middle
Ages and move into the world of the 1860s, ordered
Siamese artists to exhibit their shell carvings at the

*Box of wood inlaid with mother-of-pearl, made in
Gujerat, India, during the sixteenth or seventeenth century. Courtesy Victoria and Albert Museum, London.*

Sixteenth-century Gujerati work from India, a wooden coffer inlaid with mother-of-pearl apparently set in black mastic. Courtesy Victoria and Albert Museum, London.

Paris exhibition. "The numerous visitors to the Paris International Exhibition of 1867," wrote a contemporary, "could not fail to be struck with the mosaic pictures in mother-of-pearl, shown in the Siamese Court, representing the idol Buddha, the perfection and originality of which excited the envy of amateurs. The King of Siam, when informed of this fact, commanded the artists of his palace to execute two other mosaics, and, in order to render them more agreeable to European taste, they were made to represent the Saviour, and were presented at the close of the Exhibition to the Empress Eugènie, in order that they might adorn some Catholic chapel."

The preoccupation of the lacquer artist with Buddhist subjects is understandable. Although much shell carving went to ornament lacquer furniture for domestic use, its most striking employment was as a decoration to Buddhist temples, or *wats,* as they are called in Siam. Nowhere is this decoration employed to better effect than in the Royal Temple, Wat Prakow,, which stands within the circuit of the palace walls, and where many of the most important ceremonies of the state took place, such as the taking of the waters of allegiance. The temples of Wat Benchamabophit and Wat Rajabophit, the latter of which was built by King Chulalongkorn (1868-1910), also possess magnificent pearl inlay in lacquer.

It is difficult to refrain from superlatives when talking of Siamese lacquer. In panels such as those to which I have referred cavaliers ride through flowery glades, demigods are locked in battle, flames and dragons play lambently over the whole surface of the panel, or blooms luxuriate in a sort of vertical flower garden. In all these panels, the lacquer is reduced to a mere background, the shell inlay is everything. By comparison, the furniture and vessels in lacquer seem very tame. Besides wall decoration in temples, shell inlay was used to decorate the trays on which offerings were made, the covers of begging bowls for monks, and the book covers which kept together the long, slim pages of the holy books. Remarkable examples of the latter, and of boxes to hold books, dating from 1835, and made to the order of King Rama III, are preserved in the national library of Bangkok.

To make lacquer inlay, the surface to be ornamented—temple gate, window, or cupboard for holy books—was first planed smooth. It was next covered with lacquer several times. Then a thick layer of tough lacquer puree, mixed with the ash of tea leaves, was applied to the surface. The ornament which was to cover the surface was first done in reverse on firm paper. Then the separate parts of the design were traced from this master pattern onto pieces of mother-of-pearl. These were then cut out and stuck down on the master pattern, the whole forming a mirror image of the surface to be ornamented. The paper, with the mother-of-pearl pieces on it, was next placed on top of the sticky lacquer and forced down on it. The surface was left for a long time to dry. Then the paper was ground off and the surface polished. Only the most glowing and radiant pieces of shell could be used for this work, which required the greatest patience. Although it has been suggested that lacquer itself was derived from China, the designs used by the Siamese are obviously closely related to those in use on Indian inlay and lacquer.

Mother-of-pearl inlay, in the form of *tarsia* (inlay applied to furniture) may have existed in Rome in the work known as *opus cerostratum.* The Egyptians also worked in *tarsia,* and it probably remained in unbroken production in Egypt, while it died out in Europe. Inlaid work was made in Girgenti and Salerno after Venice had learned the art once more from the East. Pearl inlay made in Goa combines the tradition of Portuguese sixteenth- and seventeenth-century tarsia and the art of India.

Supposedly it was from Egypt that pearl shell carving and inlay were introduced, in the sixteenth century, to Palestine, where an important school of shell carving now began to develop. Damascus, which had apparently carried on the millenial old tradition of shell carving from Sumerian days, is another likely center from which it might have been imported into the Holy Land.

The shell carvers of Bethlehem, however, hold quite a different tradition. Two of them, Hany Michael Qumsiyah and Raji Qumsiyah, who are brothers and who work at mother-of-pearl carvings in Bethlehem as their forefathers have done before them, told me about the tradition in their village and how shell carving originated there:

About the twelfth century, during the Crusades, when the Crusaders came to the Holy Land, they

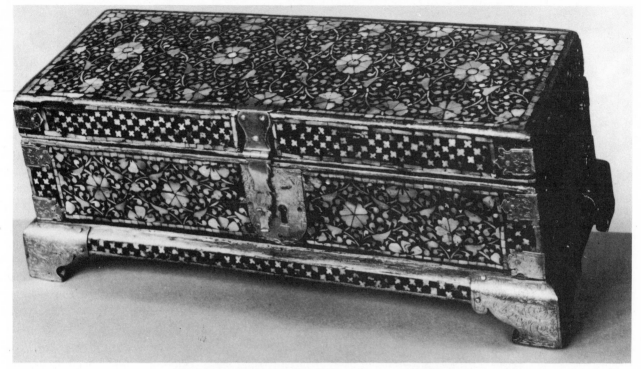

*Eighteenth-century Indian chest of wood inlaid with
mother-of-pearl. The mounts are sixteenth-century German. Victoria and Albert Museum, London.*

brought with them rosaries made from mother-of-
pearl as a gift to the Christian people in our land.
From that time onwards, our people became interested in making these articles for themselves. A cru-
sader taught the people of Bethlehem how to make
mother-of-pearl carvings, so that they could earn a
living in what was a Christian town. Since the days
of the Crusades our people have extended their carvings from rosaries to statues, nativity figures, and
religious articles such as those in the photographs
we have sent you.

Pearl shell is divided into three grades: a white
lip, from Australia, gold lip, from Indonesia or the
Philippines, and a black lip, from the Red Sea.
Formerly our people used to carve the black lip,
because it was nearest to us, and easy to get from
European traders, who bought it from Arab divers
in Saudi Arabia. However, once diving for white lip
began in Australia, our people became interested in
importing it from there, because we could use all
the raw material in a piece of shell.

The way we carve the shell is as follows: we cut
the shell from the face, and draw on it a statue, or
whatever we want to make. Then we cut it out with
a circular saw. After cutting it out, we carve it with
a knife, or fret it with a very thin saw.

Traditions can err, but there is no doubt that the
Bethlehem carvers have always been deeply in-

fluenced by Europe, if only because most of their
customers were Europeans. They still are. A peep
into Michael Qumsiyah's workshop shows that although he is still so much of an Oriental that he
sits down to work cross-legged, just as the ancient
Egyptians did, he possesses much of the equipment
that you would expect to find in a modern studio
in the West, such as an electric motor working
grindstones and buffing wheels, a power drill working rotary files through a flexible drive, calipers for
measuring the work in hand, and so forth. Although
helped by machinery, the Qumsiyah brothers have
not however abandoned the traditional skill and
meticulous craftsmanship of the Bethlehemite, as a
glance at their work will show.

As early as the fifteenth century, if not before,
ancestors of the Bethlehem carvers were already at
work supplying the pilgrim trade with souvenirs
which they could bring home to present to their
local church, or to their friends, or just to prove to
their family that they really had been to the Holy
Places. William Wey, one of the best known of
medieval pilgrims, brought back from Jerusalem

Eighteenth-century Indo-Portuguese pastoral staff, veneered with tortoiseshell, laid over a base of red paper, and inlaid with mother-of-pearl, brass, and silver studs. Courtesy Victoria and Albert Museum, London.

carvings in mother-of-pearl or olive wood from Palestine are "Franciscan work." One baptismal spoon in mother-of-pearl, now in the Victoria and Albert Museum, London, England, which shows a friar kneeling in prayer before Saint Francis of Assisi, while the Virgin appears in the clouds above, is actually described on the museum ticket as being Palestinian, early nineteenth century, and probably carved by Franciscans. The exhibit in question does bear an Italian inscription, beginning "Benedetto con il serafico padre S. Francisco. . . ." I do not feel that an inscription in Italian is sufficient to warrant the supposition that these carvings were made by immigrant friars. One writer whom I shall quote shortly says specifically that all the Christian carvers of Bethlehem could speak Italian, and speak it very well. Italian was, after al, the *lingua franca* of the Levant, down to the nineteenth century, when English took its place. Moreover, the historical evidence proves that Franciscan friars were concerned not with making carvings but with distributing them. At the present day there are some monkish carvers in Bethlehem, but when visitors stopped at the place during the eighteenth or nineteenth centuries they found all the work being carried on by the lay villagers. Such descriptions of the religious of the Holy Land as have come down to us do not suggest that they were artistic, or even that they were industrious. The only trade carried on in the Greek convent of Jerusalem was that of cobbler. Lamartine, a devout French pilgrim and Catholic writer of the nineteenth century, who would be prejudiced in favor of the monks and not against them, remarks of those of the convent of Terra Santa, "They have no other employment than the service of the church, or a walk in the gardens or on the terraces of their monasteries. They have not any books, no particular study to occupy their minds, nor are they ever engaged in any useful employment."

What was more, the continual persecution to which the friars were subjected by the Turkish authorities must have left them little leisure, or inclination, for the arts. Not merely were their churches continually pillaged, they themselves were frequently thrown into prison or martyred. In 1637, sixteen religious were carried off to Damascus and left to die in jail. Other individual martyrdoms took place. It was not unknown for a whole convent

wooden models of the Chapel of Calvary, the Church of Bethlehem, the Mount of Olives, and the Valley of Jehosaphat. None of these has survived, but they were probably very like those made in Bethlehem during the nineteenth century, meticulously accurate wooden models, inlaid with pearl shell to give artistic relief.

The suggestion has been made that the religious

to be wiped out by the plague. Kinglake, the nineteenth-century English traveler, has described for us how, as each friar in the Jerusalem convent recognized on his body the symptoms of the plague, he silently left his brothers and went to a quarantine house removed from the convent. Each day, while strength still remained, he would toll a bell to tell his brothers he was still alive, until finally, the last friar in the convent strained to catch the sound of a bell which had stopped ringing.

Bethlehem has been described for us by Father le Nau, an eighteenth-century French pilgrim. It was a well-populated village, large, and stretching east and west along a hill, with other hills ringing it round. The Christian and Muslim inhabitants lived on good terms with one another, maintaining their rights against the tyranny of the Pasha of Jerusalem, with the help of the Bedouins, with whom they had a close alliance. "When angered, the villagers become terrible," Le Nau tells us. "The Christians were formerly mainly Greeks, but the charity of the Fathers of the Holy Land, and their life, which is more exemplary than that of the religious men of the other Christian nations of the East, has converted a great number of them. And I believe that there are scarcely less than fifty good Catholic families, all following the Roman rite. There is hardly anyone amongst these Catholics who does not know Italian, and can speak it without an interpreter. Their livelihood, which is that of the other Christians, and even of the Muslims, is to make rosaries. These are blessed in the Holy Places. They are sent to Europe and the pilgrims take care of the distribution. The best workmen make beautiful crosses, and models of the complete church of the Holy Sepulchre, and also the whole church of Bethlehem, of the Holy Grotto and the Holy Sepulchre with such exactitude that not even a pillar, or even the

Seventeenth- or eighteenth-century Damascus cabinet decorated with marquetry (intarsia) of mother-of-pearl. Courtesy Victoria and Albert Museum, London.

Chess and backgammon board of wood inlaid with
marquetry (tarsia) *of tortoiseshell and mother-of-pearl.*
Courtesy Victoria and Albert Museum, London.

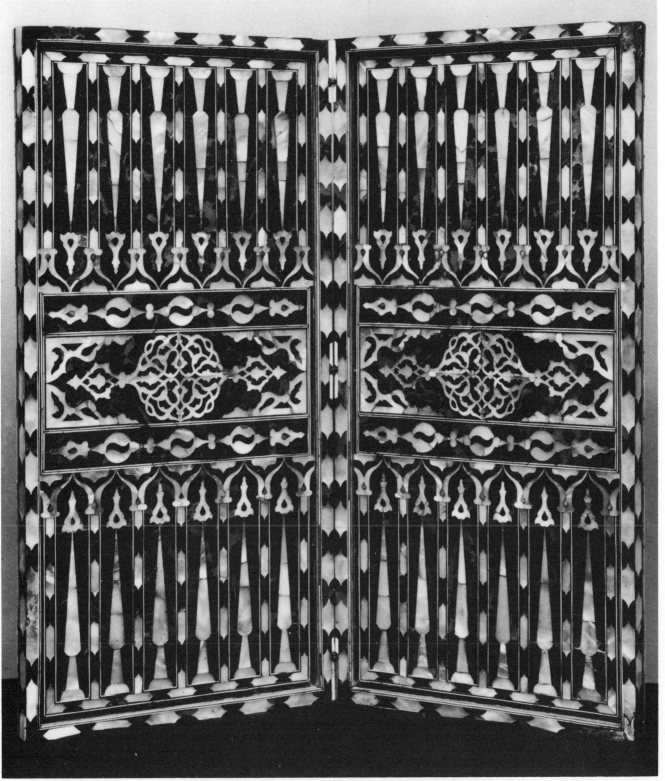

Nineteenth-century Syrian chess and backgammon board of wood with marquetry (tarsia) of mother-of-pearl, tortoiseshell, and ivory. Probably made in Damascus. Courtesy Victoria and Albert Museum, London.

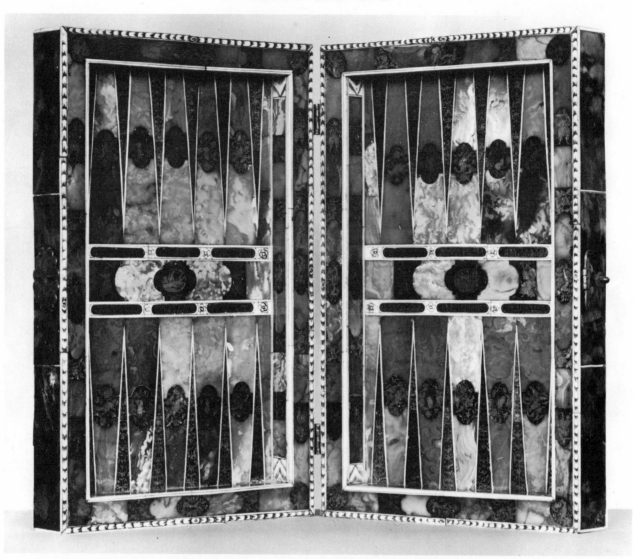

Nineteenth-century Syrian chess and backgammon board of wood with marquetry (tarsia) of mother-of-pearl, tortoiseshell, and ivory.

least column, is missing." Another eighteenth-century observer describes Bethlehem as "very agreeably situated, built on the top of a middling-sized hill, surrounded by hills and valleys planted with olive trees, figs, and vines, which produce very excellent wine, with lovely fields which produce wheat in abundance."

From these descriptions, it might seem as though life in Bethlehem was idyllic. A glance at the Latin convent, however, would soon dispel this idea. It was surrounded by fortress like walls, with a portal that would have done service as a town gate. These

fortifications were not intended for show, but as a protection for the monks from the turbulent villagers. The Bethlehemites did not quarrel about religion, like the inhabitants of other parts of Palestine. Whether they were Turks, Arabs, Moors, Greeks, or Latin Christians mattered not a whit to any of them. They all lived quietly in the same village without any quarrels about belief. There were plenty of other occasions for quarrels, however. They insisted on their right to hire out horses to the pilgrims passing through and to extract *caffar* from them, a sort of blackmail canonized by centuries of usage. They all belonged to one of two rival factions, known as the "red ensign" and the "white ensign." The official ruler of Bethlehem was the governor of Jaffa. The distance from authority encouraged the Bethlehemites to persevere in their already turbulent courses. They kept up a constant feud with the inhabitants of Jerusalem, or with the townspeople of Hebron. These feuds produced a bloody toll of casualties, and occasionally the men of Hebron would hew down the olive groves of Bethlehem—thus producing more raw material for the manufacture of crucifixes and rosaries.

"None suffer more from these wicked Bethlehemites," a Swedish traveler called Hasselquist

Table decorated with mother-of-pearl and tortoiseshell. Syrian, probably from Damascus, work of the nineteenth century. Courtesy Victoria and Albert Museum, London.

Eighteenth- or nineteenth-century model in wood and mother-of-pearl of the Church of the Holy Sepulchre in Jerusalem. Probably made in Bethlehem. Courtesy British Museum, London.

Model of the Church of the Holy Sepulchre with the top removed. Courtesy British Museum, London.

Another model of approximately the same date. Courtesy British Museum, London.

wrote in 1750, "than the monks, their neighbors. These would be happy, if they were safe by being shut up within the walls of their convent, but they every day apprehend being attacked in their own chambers, by these robbers. They surprise the monks, either to obtain provisions, which like most robbers, they want continually, or attack and force them to buy a quantity of Paternosters [rosaries] models of the grave of Christ, crosses, and other wares of this kind, which is the only employ of all the inhabitants of this village. Of these they have so large a stock in Jerusalem that the Procurator [a convent official] told me he had to the value of 15,000 piasters of relics in the magazine [store room] of the convent; a sum which one would scarcely believe could be expended in such things. An incredible quantity of them go yearly to all the Roman Catholic countries in Europe, but most to Spain and Portugal. Great part is bought by the Turks, who come yearly for these commodities. A number is yearly sent by the monks in Jerusalem to be given as presents to the patrons of their order;

and these are best paid for by other presents they receive in return. No Pilgrim goes away without carrying with him a store of these wares, and therefore the making of these holy things is a constant and certain employ for the inhabitants of Jerusalem and Bethlehem, with which they may drive on a monopoly as lasting as the Dutch do, with nutmeg and cinammon. The dexterity and art with which they make these things, especially the Paternosters, and a Bull from the Pope, which grants indulgences to those who have Paternosters brought from these holy places, are circumstances which add to their credit."

When Haselquist visited the monks they had been besieged in their monastery so long by the Bethlehemites, with nothing to eat except the salt fish that they normally kept for fast days, that they had acquired scurvy. The Swedish physician prescribed for them a diet of the watercress which grew near the Well of Solomon.

"The Bethlemite Arabs are the most detestable race of those countries," wrote the French traveler

Lamartine, "always at war with their neighbors, or putting the Latin monastery of Bethlehem under ransom." The villagers kept up a close relationship with the Bedouins of the desert, led by bandit chiefs like Abou Ghosh, so that they could join forces to kidnap American or European pilgrims on their way to Jerusalem and hold them to ransom. In 1834, Ibrahim Pasha, the Egyptian conqueror of Syria, tired of their turbulent ways, massacred the Muslim inhabitants of the village and destroyed their quarter. He also disarmed the Christian inhabitants who, however, remained dangerous. Murray, in his handbook for Palestine travelers of 1858, warns his readers that any European pilgrim who displays too close an admiration of the beauty of the Bethlehem girls, which is very remarkable, is likely to be left weltering in his blood by their menfolk.

The rosaries, crosses, and medals which the villagers carved, together with their work in bituminous schist from Moses' tomb (Neby Musa) and their models and crucifixes made from olive wood from Mount Olivet, inlaid with nacre from the Red Sea, were given away to pilgrims by the Friars of the Franciscan convent of St. Saviours, or Terra Santa as it was also called. The convent was a sort of hotel for all visitors of good standing from America or Europe. Not only Catholics but also Protestants stayed there during their pilgrimage, making a present at the end equivalent to the time they had stopped. John Madox, an English pilgrim of 1834, described how he was offered a choice of rooms, or rather cell, "I took one in a quiet situation, having a paved court, and my servant had the room adjoining. Here I was settled as long as it might suit me, in a room fifteen feet in length, by eight in width, arched and rather damp; the window was without glass, but had iron bars and wire instead; there was no chimney; a cupboard and table, two seats and a chair were brought to me, and a bed was formed of boards placed upon irons, at the height of a foot from the plaster floor.

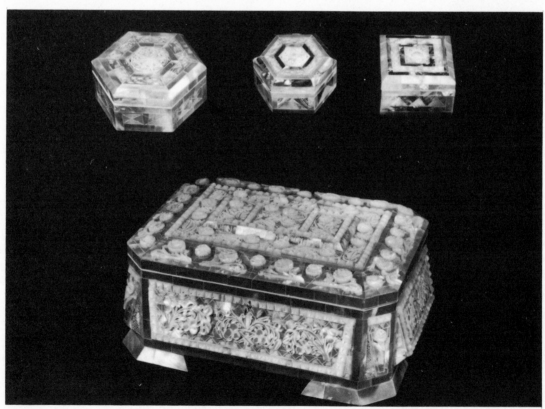

Traditional-style boxes for jewelry made from mother-of-pearl by Hany Qumsiyah. Courtesy Hany M. Qumsiyah and Brothers, Bethlehem, Israel.

Siamese tazza *of the nineteenth century inlaid with mother-of-pearl in a bird-and-flower design. Courtesy Victoria and Albert Museum, London.*

These, with a large jar of water, and a pewter wash-hand basin, completed the furniture. I rejoiced to get into so clean a place, with an attentive and good servant, speaking Italian, belonging to the convent."

So customary was the presentation of these pearl rosaries and crosses by the monks to their visitors, that even when the convent was in quarantine, because of the plague, they were let down, in a basket, to Lamartine and his party, as they halted in their journey across the desert under the walls of the convent. "We received from them,' 'he wrote, "a supply of crosses, rosaries, and other pious curiosities, with which they have always their magazines abundantly supplied." Lamartine handed over two thousand piasters as a return present—about the price of twenty horses. He did more, when the Arab inhabitants of Bethlehem begged him to intercede with Ibrahim Pasha to have their taxes reduced, he promised to

put in a good word for them. "On one condition however, that they would respect the Europeans, the pilgrims and all the monasteries of Bethlehem, and of the Desert of St. John, and that if they committed the slightest violation of the abodes of those poor monks, Ibrahim Pasha had formed the resolution to exterminate them to the very last man." The Arabs did not keep their promise, with the result that, as Lamartine had warned them, they were wiped out by the Egyptian conqueror.

Many of the carvings were on sale in Bethlehem itself, where an American traveler of 1854, Bayard Taylor, remarked, "The bazaars are poor, compared with those of other Oriental cities of the same size, and the principal trade seems to be in rosaries, both Turkish and Christian, crosses, seals, amulets, and pieces of the Holy Sepulchre." Most of the selling, however, was done in Jerusalem itself, in the shops of the city, or among the teeming crowds of pilgrims

*Eighteenth-century Siamese lacquer cabinet inlaid with
shell. Courtesy Victoria and Albert Museum, London.*

at the door of the Church of the Holy Sepulchre. Jerusalem was only a two-hour journey from Bethlehem for someone mounted on a horse or mule, and many carvers took their products there and turned salesmen.

"If you would make any purchases," wrote the witty English traveler Alexander Kinglake, who visited Jerusalem in 1834, "you must go again to the Church doors, and when you inquire for the manufactures of the place, you find that they consist of double-blessed beads, and sanctified shells. These last are the favorite tokens, which the pilgrims carry off with them. The shell is graven, or rather scratched, on the white side, with a rude drawing of the Blessed Virgin, or of the Crucifixion, or some other Scriptural subject; having passed this stage, it goes into the hands of a priest, by him it is subjected to some process for rendering it efficacious against the schemes of our ghostly enemies; the manufacture is then complete, and is deemed to be fit for use."

A traveler with a much less scoffing attitude toward religion, and a deep admiration for both the Latin and the Greek churches, the Honorable

English parlormaid's tray, nineteenth century, made from papier-mâché, lacquered and inlaid with mother-of-pearl. Courtesy Victoria and Albert Museum, London.

Still life by J. de Heem. This seventeenth-century Dutch picture apparently preserves a form of decoration not represented by any surviving specimen. The curve of the shell has been opened and carved into a knight's helm, otherwise the natural striped brown and cream decoration of the outside is intact. No collector, least of all a Dutchman, would ever really treat his treasures in the casual way of this picture anymore than he would leave expensive drinking glasses and silver flagons where they might fall down at any minute. Courtesy Wallace Collection.

Robert Curzon, described just what happened to the shell crucifixes and rosaries once the pilgrims had bought them. "We went to the church of the Holy Sepulchre," he noted in 1834, "descending the hill from the convent, and then down a flight of narrow steps into a small paved court, one side of which is occupied by the Gothic front of the church. The court was full of people selling beads and crucifixes and other holy ware. We had to wait some time, till the Turkish doorkeepers came to unlock the door, as they keep the keys of the church, which is only open on certain days, except to votaries of distinction. There is a hole in the door, through which the pilgrims gave quantities of things to the monks inside to be laid upon the sepulchre."

Because a pilgrimage was such a dangerous bus-

Engraved shell plaque from Ur of the Chaldees. The sharp, angular lines which join toe, hand, and elbow indicate that a straight graver or burin was used to make this engraving. A style would have swept round these naturally curved surfaces.

ness, every pilgrim brought with him his shroud, which he dipped in the Pool of Siloam and had blessed at the Holy Sepulchre. They also acquired, as Kinglake, tells us, "sundry rosaries and ornaments made of pearl oyster shell—all which are defenses against the powers of darkness." That these preparations were by no means redundant can be seen from incidents such as the massacre in the Church of the Holy Sepulchre in 1833, when during the performance of the annual "miracle" of the Holy Fire, which was supposed to issue from the openings of the tomb, the congregation inside the church panicked and trampled one another to death. Four hundred pilgrims perished as the Egyptian guards forced them back into the church with fixed bayonets. Afterwards Kinglake — who had only escaped from the scene of horror by scrambling over great heaps of dead, saw the bodies of the pilgrims laid out in the convent courtyard, each with his pearl shell amulet. "These pearl shells," Kinglake shrewdly surmises, "are, I imagine, the scallop shell

of romance, for there are no scallops to be found here." Throughout the Middle Ages, the scallop shell, worn on the hat, had been the badge of pilgrims. It was not to be found in the Holy Land, though it could be gathered on the other very popular pilgrimage to St. James of Compostella. Gradually the shell badge came to be regarded as not merely a sign of pilgrimage, but the most effective of all charms against any possible evil. From the fifteenth century onward, German pilgrims had been carrying back to Europe souvenirs of the Holy Land, including natural objects such as stones and shells. Carvings of scallop shells in mother-of-pearl from the Red Sea would no doubt have been regarded as a particularly potent charm. So would a religious medal carved in the same substance. If it is assumed that pearl shell carving began in Bethlehem during the late Middle Ages, then it might be possible to trace the beginning of European pearl shell carvings to this source. Significantly, nacre carving begins in Germany, where pilgrimages to the Holy Land were popular.

The belief in the efficacy of the shell carvings as an amulet remained in full force until just before the first World War among the simple Russian peasants who bulked so largely among the pilgrims. Members of the Eastern and Greek churches had always outnumbered the Latins. For the Russian *moujik,* the pilgrimage to Jerusalem was the climax of his whole life. His faith in the effiicacy of everything to do with the Holy Land was boundless. To visit it, he had begged from door to door, collected dried crusts in a sack for his victuals on the voyage from Odessa, perhaps even sold or mortgaged his land. An adventurous Englishman named Stephen Graham, who made the pilgrimage in 1911, disguised as a Rusian peasant, along with many Russians, wrote of one of his companions, "The pilgrim had been many times to the Grave, and he showed me a carved baptism cross which he had taken in with him to the inner sanctuary. When he got back to his native village, greater gift than this cross, thus sanctified, could not be within his power. It would be something to outlast life and the world itself, a token around the neck of the wearer when dead— the same token around his neck on the final day of resurrection. For the peasant goes to Jerusalem in order that he may die in a certain sort of way in Russia." Pilgrims would buy objects needed for their own deathbed, which included death-caps, shrouds, "pictures of the Crucified one cut on tablets of mother-of-pearl," and pearl crosses which would be placed in their hands after death. They also bought similar pilgrim's ware with the money which had been entrusted to them by other villagers, sometimes starving to death by the banks of the Jordan rather than spending the sacred trust imposed on them.

7

The Gates of Heaven:
Mother-of-Pearl Carving in Europe

The impulse which produced the birth of nacre carving in Europe has been seen by Gustav Pazaurek, the great German art historian, as emanating, not from Bethlehem, but from China. He has pointed to the similarity of some of the designs used on medieval European pearl shell carvings and those worked by the Chinese, and suggested that imported Chinese nacre carvings may have originated the art in Europe. Other factors to which mother-of-pearl shell carving may be attributed are, he says, the difficulty of obtaining ivory, the unsuitable nature of the substitutes used, such as mammoth tusks, and the passion of fifteenth-century Italy for cameos, first of shell, notably from the shell of the giant snail, and finally from mother-of-pearl.

Pazaurek himself admits, however, that early mother-of-pearl carvers were completely preoccupied with sacred material. The carvings made were used for altar and church decoration, or, like those in the Thomas Whitcombe Green collection, in the Victoria and Albert Museum, London, they were intended as rosary beads or pendants. The subjects of these carvings include the presentation of the Virgin, her coronation, annunciation, the birth of Christ, the adoration of the Magi, scenes from the life of Christ which include the passion, the Mount of Olives, the carrying of the cross, the crucifixion, the taking down from the cross, the resurrection, the Gregorian Mass, the death of the Virgin, and various legends of Saints, such as Christopher, Catherine, George, Barbara, and Sebastian. The wholly religious nature of these themes seems to bear out my contention that early nacre carving was associated with the Holy Places, that some of the carvings we have may actually have been carved in Palestine, while others were made in Germany and the Low Countries, perhaps from shells brought home by pilgrims a souvenirs.

In technique the carvings are very varied. Some are deeply, some very lightly carved. One or two have the figures cut out completely in silhouette, while others have the design carved *ajouré,* that is, with gaps cut out in the shell with a piercing saw, so as to make the rest of the design stand out in greater relief. The silhouette carvings are of particular interest, because they make it possible to relate the very early carvings to the work of the gun stock maker, which will be examined in a moment. Silhouette carvings of this sort, such as the portrait heads which begin to appear toward the end of the medieval period, could have formed part of the decoration of a gun stock of some dark wood. Because of the thin nature of the material it is only carved on one side. Some gilding and traces of color are still visible on a few carvings, but most of them were left in their natural state. The metal settings which enclosed these carvings, which were almost certainly of gold or silver, have long been removed and melted down. Much of the work may be assumed

119

*The connection between the Holy Places of Jerusalem
and German fifteenth-century nacre-carving is emphasized in this shell, which appears to depict a pilgrim
(note the staff and scrip) treading down the dragon of
unrighteousness while standing upon a monogram of
the Holy Name. Courtesy Victoria and Albert Museum,
London.*

*German carving of the fifteenth century. The left-hand
medal represents the baptism of Christ by St. John the
Baptist; the right-hand one is the dead Christ attended
by angels. Both are very similar in shape, method of
suspension, and subject to the holy medals which continue to be made in Palestine in our own day. Courtesy
British Museum, London.*

Christ carrying the cross. Fifteenth-century German carving. Courtesy Victoria and Albert Museum, London.

German carvings of the fifteenth century in mother-of-pearl. Large completely carved shells such as the one showing the Crucifixion (on the right) are a frequent feature in traditional Holy Land pearl shell sculpture. Courtesy Victoria and Albert Museum, London.

to have been carved by goldsmiths, except in a few areas, such as Burgundy, where mother-of-pearl was not admitted as part of the materials which a goldsmith might use. Much of what has survived is German, probably South German work, though there are some datable carvings apparently made in Prague under Sigismund, around 1406. One piece, dated 1465, was made and signed by a goldsmith of Prague named Darlin. A small altar bears the date 1494 and the Salzburg hallmark together with the maker's name, Perchtold, and is distinctly German work. The heyday of nacre carving in Germany lasted from the middle of the fifteenth to the middle of the sixteenth century. After that it degenerates into coarse peasant art.

The Renaissance saw the rise of the mother-of-pearl portrait. Nacre competed with boxwood, ivory, and cameo in this field. There are several portrait carvings from France of the middle of the sixteenth century, including a head of Henri III in the Louvre and Henri IV in the Bibliotheque Nationale. In Nuremberg, many portaits of princes and prominent citizens were made in mother-of-pearl. Hans Keller (1575–1600) is associated with many of them. He also set work in silver for Wurzburg and Frankfurt.

Some very fine work in shell was done by Italian ivory carvers, such as the master I. Cognia, who made a signed portrait of Rudolph II as well as of the Duke and Duchess of Ferrara in 1566. Some of the later Hapsburgs were portrayed on giant snail shells, and there are several well-executed

German fifteenth-century pearl shell carvings. Left, The Last Supper; center, the dead Christ; right, Saint Veronica with the shroud of Christ showing the holy face. These themes would have served ideally for souvenir medals brought back from the Holy Sepulchre in Jeruslaem. Were they copied from carvings made in Palestine and brought by pilgrims to Europe? Courtesy Victoria and Albert Museum, London.

Fifteenth-century German mother-of-pearl carving. The subjects are: top, the Gifts of the Magi, bottom, left, the Annunciation, and right, St. George and the Dragon. The latter theme at least suggests an English provenance. Vicoria and Albert Museum, London.

These fifteenth- or sixteenth-century German carvings in mother-of-pearl show the development of the themes of the art from religious to secular. The top carvings illustrate religious topics, such as the Crucifixion and the Holy Family, the Coronation of the Virgin, and the Descent from the Cross. At the bottom there are two portraits and a medal worn by some Renaissance revolutionary with "Strike Judith" on it. Courtesy Victoria and Albert Museum, London.

heads from as late as the end of the seventeenth century. One portrait of Gustavus Adophus, dating from 1633, is signed "W.Z."

Much of the inlay made in mother-of-pearl during this period is not true inlay, it was simply stuck on to the wooden base, and has consequently worn very badly. Elias Geyer, who was particularly fond of working with shell, began setting it in ornaments of gold and silver. There are several examples of Elias Geyer's work in the Green Vault collection in Dresden. An early renaissance font at Nuremberg, enriched with mother-of-pearl, is the work of a goldsmith named Flötner.

Friedrich Hilleband (who died in 1608) made composite sculptures from pearl shell, such as birds, where the body was formed from a whole nautilus shell and the rest of the sculpture carried out in gold or silver plate. Georg Barst and the Jamnitzer family, which included Christoph, Wenzel, and Hans, were making goblets and other ornaments

A group of fifteenth- and sixteenth-century German carvings of unequal merit and varying subjects. They depict from left to right: the Virgin, the martyrdom of Saint Sebastian, two patron saints, Christ's entry into Jerusalem (a station of the cross), the adoration of the Magi, Christ carrying the cross (a station of the cross), a portrait, the Annunciation, and a head, probably that of Minerva. Victoria and Albert Museum, London.

at the end of the sixteenth century. Other artists at work include Elias Lencker, who died in Nuremberg in 1591 and who is famous for his use of shell in a Calvary, Nicolaus Schmidt, and Hans Straub, who worked in Berlin.

Special mention must be made of the work of the gunstock maker. At a time when mother-of-pearl had lost its leading role and had been degraded to serving as a mere adjunct for furniture, a background for goldsmith's work, and an ornament for small boxes, musical instruments, and gaming boards, such as the famous chessboard in the National Museum, Munich, the oval discs and square inlay let into the stocks of artistically decorated weapons, with their delightful scenes of the chase, or subjects drawn from mythology, form a welcome relief to the rather heavy portraiture of the time.

South German crucifix in pearl shell, fifteenth or sixteenth century. Courtesy author's collection. Photograph courtesy Stella Mayes Reed.

A firearm cost so much in the sixteenth century that those who could afford one could also afford to have it covered with the most princely ornament. This included not merely chasing and engraving the barrel and inlaying it with gold and silver, but the ornamentation of the whole gun stock with inlay of pearl, stag's horn, and ivory. It is unfortunate that the work of the sixteenth-century stock maker is almost always anonymous. Carvers of no great merit did their work side by side with artists of real distinction, who are responsible for many pieces of really masterly inlay. All the decoration of the gun, apart from what was on the lock and barrel, was carried on in the gun stocker's workshop by men he employed. Who they were is mostly a matter for speculation. All that is known about them is that they drew on the prints of contemporary masters, such as the de Buys, Peter Flötner, Virgil Solis, Etienne Delaune, Jost Amman, and Adriaen and Hans Collaert, for their ornament. It is extremely significant that the only identifiable gunstock decorator, Johannes Sadeler, afterwards became an engraver.

Other gun-stock makers attempted to move out of what was essentially a craft occupation. They included the most famous of all shell-carving families, the Belkeins, who are also noticed in another chapter for their work on the nautilus shell. Jérémie Belquin was a maker of inlay for arquebuses (a *monteur d'arquebuses,* is his description in contemporary records). He moved to Utrecht in 1604 because of the religious troubles in Germany. Soon the Belquins moved again, this time to Amsterdam. Jérémie's son, Jean, became an engraver on mother-of-pearl and a maker of pearl shell inlay in the same city. One of Jean's sons, Jan, seems to have worked almost exclusively in nautilus shell. Something is said about him elsewhere. Cornelis Bellekin, the most famous of all the family, must have been another son, or a nephew, of Jean's. Although he carved nautilus shells as well as mother-of-pearl he managed to excel in both media. Cornelis made portraits, such as his two portrait medallions of William and Mary, which are carved on mother-of-pearl and provided with tortoiseshell frames. He also portrayed Queen Anne. Other aspects of his work include what the Dutch connoisseurs of this period called "Farmer's Joys," scenes of rustic merrymaking. He also worked at Biblical scenes,

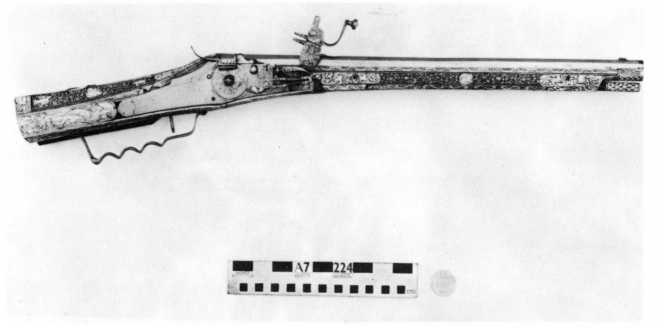

*Short wheel lock gun. German, possibly Saxon. Dated
1586, this piece is inlaid with mother-of-pearl insets
showing animals. Courtesy Tower of London.*

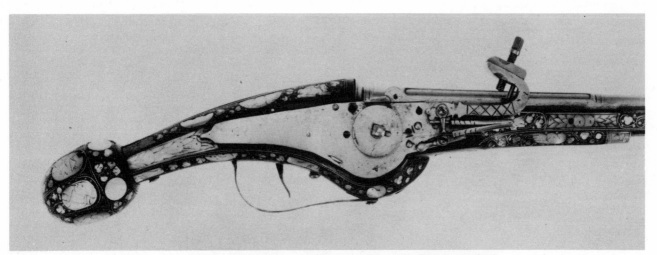

*Short wheel lock gun. German, possibly Saxon. Dated
1586. The mother-of-pearl decoration has worn, while
that in stag's horn is still intact. This factor may have
produced the virtual abandonment of mother-of-pearl
in gun decoration. Courtesy Tower of London.*

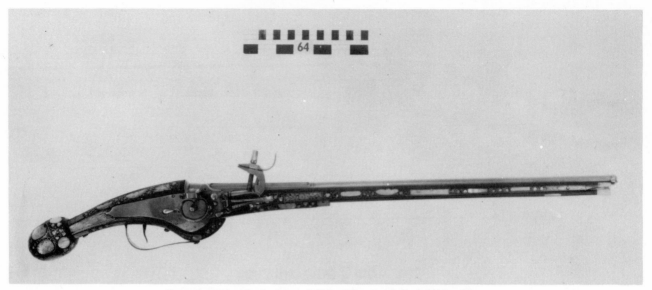

Lorraine pistol of about 1610. The stock is inlaid with mother-of-pearl, stag's horn, and brass wire. Courtesy Tower of London.

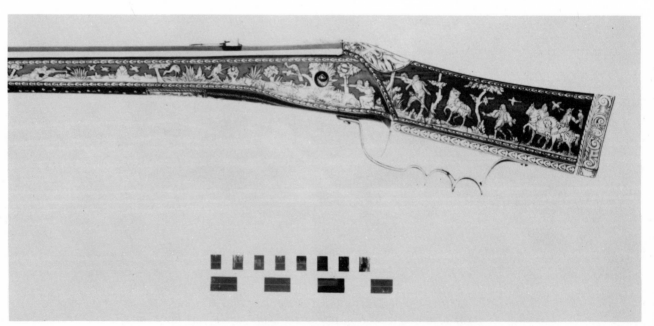

Wheel lock rifle, German, about 1580, with mother-of-pearl inlay. Courtesy Tower of London.

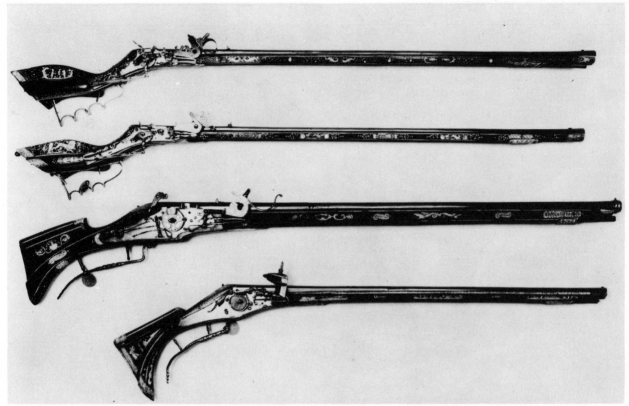

Wheel lock rifles, two of which are by Tschinke and date from the 1620s, inlaid with mother-of-pearl plaques. Courtesy Tower of London.

such as the "Flight Into Egypt," subjects taken from classical mythology, and even a few subjects drawn from contemporary life, such as the "Meeting of the Estates of Cambrai."

Except for Jean Gaulette, the other nacre carvers of the seventeenth century are much less rewarding than are the Belkeins. Foremost is J. Hercules, a delightful portraistist known to me only from one intarsia figure, portraying Frederick III of Denmark, in court dress of the mid-1660s, which is preserved in the Royal Danish Collection at Rosenborg Castle.

A much better known figure in work of exactly the same style, engraved pearl shell mounted on slate, is Dirk Van Ryswyk (1596–1679). This artist has some very warm admirers, including Sterck, who made a special study of his work. Ryswyk drew his own designs for the carvings which he made, and they suffered in the process, for he was a much less skillful draughtsman than a carver. On occasion, for example, he would

juxtapose a large vase of flowers with a ridiculously small monkey. This is a mistake which the Belkiens would never have made. His able, but rather heavy flower pieces are his most successful work.

Special mention must be made of Gaulette, a French carver who produced two superb medallions depicting the Triumph of Coriolanus, now in the Victoria and Albert Museum, London. Besides the carvers whom I have discussed there are others known only by name. They include Jochem Kuhne, from Bremen, who worked in Amsterdam; Evans, with his very British-sounding name, and Roeners, who both carried on their art in the same city.

Little mother-of-pearl work of any note was produced in the eighteenth century. Jan Bernard Barckhuyzen (1684–1760), who was a seal cutter and die cutter at the Amsterdam mint, was a productive artist. He carved many Biblical, mythological, and allegorical scenes, but his work has been condemned, on the great authority of Van Seters, as

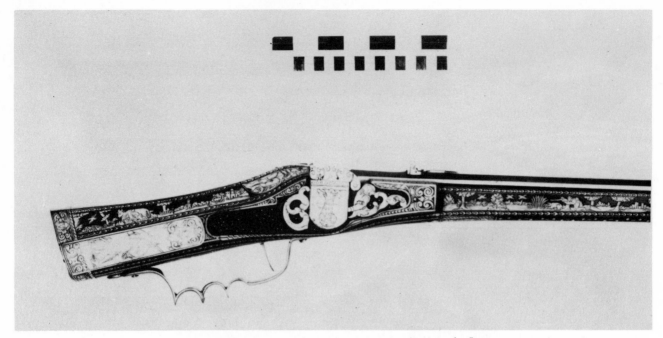

Seventeenth-century rifle with enclosed wheel lock. In-laid with mother-of-pearl. Courtesy Tower of London.

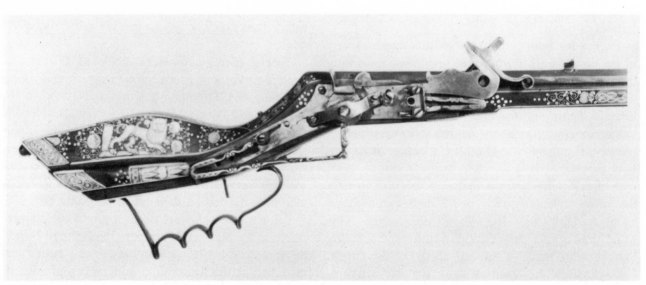

Rifle by Tschinke, Silesian gunmaker, dated around 1620. The butt and stock are inlaid with mother-of-pearl. Courtesy Tower of London.

Butt of French short match lock gun, of about 1590. The whole stock is ornamented with engraved mother-of-pearl panels of birds and animals. Like many other treasures of the Tower Armouries, this gun was collected by the American amateur W. V. Hearst. Courtesy Tower of London.

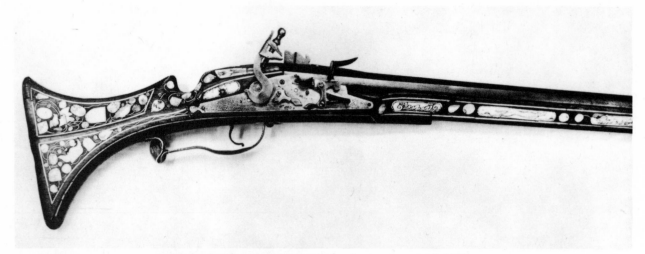

Flintlock musket, English or Dutch, dated around 1600.
Courtesy Tower of London.

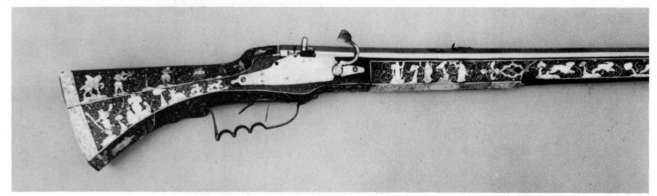

Swiss matchlock of 1619 with mother-of-pearl inlay.
Courtesy Tower of London.

lacking the refinement and charm of the Belkiens, and showing occasional clumsiness, where the shell has not been sufficiently worked over. Like the Belkiens, he often carved the tops of tobacco boxes. other pearl shell carvers working during the eighteenth century include Johannes Christian Konsé, born in Frankfurt in 1700, who worked as a goldsmith and seal cutter in Amsterdam, and Cornelis la Motte.

To pass from mother-of-pearl carving in the early eighteenth century to the work of the nineteenth is to go from art to industrial application. In Italy, mother-of-pearl was worked up in large quantities, chiefly around Naples. First the pearl shells would have the horny outer layers (the *periostracum*) ground away. The handworker would press them against a grindstone, which revolved in a trough of water. Once the shell was ground smooth, it would be sawed into suitable pieces for the carvers. Next the craftman would coat the parts of the shell which were to stand out in relief with wax, and then leave it in an acid bath. Then the carving would be washed, and worked up with files, drills, burins, and engravers. The acid discolored the shell and also weakened it. The only function it served was to hasten on the work. When the hollows left by the acid had been carved into shape and all traces of carving removed by scrapers, the work was polished with a linen rag dipped in emery powder. Specially shaped sticks, cut from limewood and coated with emery powder, were forced into the crevices where the rag could not penetrate. A

Powder flask of ebony, inlaid with decoration in stag's horn and mother-of-pearl. In the center a man is playing the flute or fife. German, dated 1616, Tower of London.

Jean Bellequin, "Mars Smoking." Rijksmuseum, Amsterdam, Holland.

Mother-of-pearl carving by Jean Bellequin of the Battle of Leckerbeetjen. Rijksmuseum, Amsterdam, Holland.

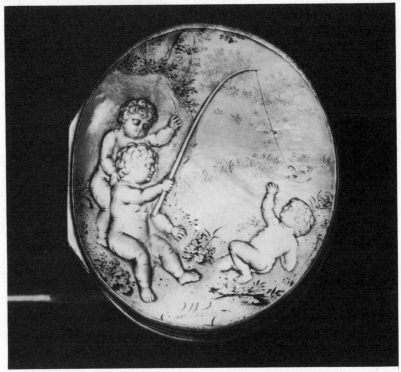

*Mother-of-pearl cover by Cornelis Bellekin for a silver
tobacco box. Rijksmuseum, Amsterdam, Holland.*

*"The Triumph of Coriolanus" by Jean Gaulette, seven-
teenth-century French carver. Courtesy Victoria and
Albert Museum, London.*

Signed and dated panel of slate inlaid with mother-of-pearl by Derik van Rijswick, 1665. Courtesy Victoria and Albert Museum, London.

rics, their products are markedly less attractive than those of the hand shell carvers of the early part of the century, such as those in France, for example, who produced many charming utilitarian objects.

In America and England during this period shell carvings were for use rather than just for show. Nacre was carved into many 'fancy articles,' which included knife handles, studs, fans, book covers, and card cases. The biggest demand was always for pearl buttons, which still take the bulk of all pearl shell carved. Much pearl shell was used for inlay by Cabinet makers, piano manufacturers, and pa-

Panel of slate inlaid with mother-of-pearl. The small label in the corner reads "Derik van Rijswick drew and engraved this in the year 1665." Note the diminutive parrot dwarfed by the vase, which in turn is dwarfed by the flowers. Rijswick's undoubted talent as an engraver and carver was considerably greater than his power to design. Courtesy Victoria and Albert Museum, London.

further polish was given with the finest powdered tripoli, and then tripoli powder and sulphuric acid, well mixed together, were appiled on the end of a cork to the carving. A final wash in soap and water was given to the work. By the nineteenth century the last polish applied to nacre was given with a machine-driven buffing wheel, covered with felt and charged with powdered tripoli. Other polishing powders in use include calcined sulphate of iron and whiting mixed with water.

It is not surprising that processes which included so many mechanical steps, in which the efforts of the individual artist could have no purpose, resulted in a product which was lifeless and unlovely. Although the Italian carvers experimented unceasingly with new uses for mother-of-pearl, making it into book covers and sequins which were sewn onto fab-

J. B. Barckhuyzen, one of the last masters of mother-of-pearl, carved this scene of "Esther before Ahasue-rus" in the eighteenth century. Courtesy Victoria and Albert Museum, London.

pier-mâché workers. Pen holders, carved brooches, earrings, buckles, sleeve links, small boxes, stamp cases, covers for memorandum books, baskets with metal handles, buttons, ring trays, standishes, and very many other articles were made from wood or papier-mâché inlaid with nacre.

At the beginning of the nineteenth century, Birmingham was the center of the shell working industry in Britain. By 1879, however, French imports of shell had reached 1,500 tons a year, the same amount that Britain imported, and the United States had become such a formidable competitor to England that Birmingham had to lay off many of its workers. Fluctuations in the value of pearl shell also helped to disrupt the English shell-carving industries. The thick pearl shells from Manila, Singapore, and Australia, which the cutlers of Sheffield used for "scales," as the two halves of a knife handle were called, varied in price from £ 60 to £ 600 a ton between 1829 and 1879. So wildly did prices move that black lip shell, which had been imported to Birmingham in 1864, and which had suddenly lost its appeal to the fashionable public, had to be buried to get rid of it. Only a few years later black lip became fashionable once more, and was in such great demand that people paid to be allowed to dig up their neighbors' gardens in the

hope that they might find some of the precious shell. One Birmingham citizen even proposed tearing down the town hall, which had been built upon trenches filled with discarded shell. "It would almost pay, at present prices," he remarked.

Besides mother-of-pearl, other iridescent shells, such as the "green snail," or *turbo olearius*, were used for ornamental inlay in Birmingham. Slices of shell were ground down to a thin surface. Then a considerable number of them were cemented together with glue, and the design to be inlaid was drawn up on the outer plate. The combined plates were then clamped in a vice and either cut out as one plate, with a fine saw, or filed into shape. Drilling was also used to assist this operation. Then the pieces of shell were separated by being thrown into warm water, which dissolved the glue. The cut-out shapes were now ready to be applied to the article which they were intended to decorate. This could be either cast iron, papier-mâché, wood, or some other material. The inlayer began work by cleaning the surface to be decorated, and blackened it with a coat of varnish and lamp black. When this had dried, a coat of japan (a kind of varnish made from shellac) was spread on it. While it was still tacky, the cut-out pieces of shell inlay, which had been formed into the shape of leaves, roses, or other decorative elements, were placed here and there on the surface to make up a pattern, and then pressed into the japan so that they adhered. The piece to be decorated was then baked in an oven till dry. Then more layers of varnish were laid on and allowed to dry. The surface was now scraped down with a knife, and the pearl inlay smoothed with a pumice stone and water. Finally the whole piece of inlay would be polished with powdered pumice stone and water.

Occasionally the inlay worker would proceed to gild the lily by drawing in the details of the veins and stems of the foliage represented by the inlay, in size, gilding them by pressing gold leaf into the pattern, and rubbing off the superfluous leaf with a piece of silk. The part of the design which was left ungilded would then be painted in color, and finally covered with a coat of clear varnish.

Aaron Jennens and John Bettridge, two English factory owners, had patented a process for making pearl inlay which they are supposed to have learned about owing to its invention by one of their

*Clasp knife of silver gilt and white mother-of-pearl,
encrusted with gold and stained mother-of-pearl. The
French Royal Cipher and coat of arms are introduced
into the decoration. The blade is stamped "Michaut,"
at Paris. French, second half of the eighteenth century.
Courtesy Wallace Collection.*

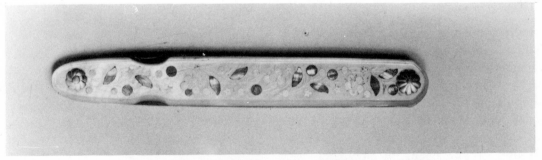

*French, late eighteenth-century penknife of white
mother-of-pearl, encrusted with gold and stained
mother-of-pearl. Courtesy Wallace Collection.*

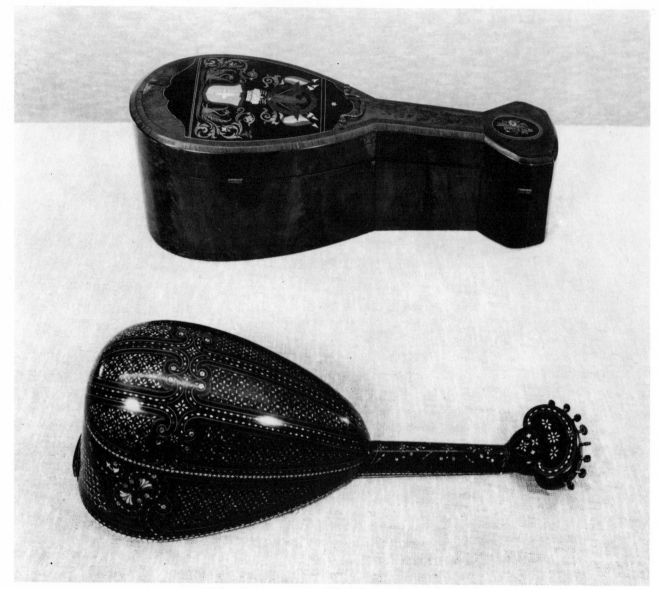

Mandolin and case inlaid with mother-of-pearl. Perhaps nineteenth century. The flowered pattern suggests Venice or Girgenti work. Courtesy Victoria and Albert Museum, London.

workmen, George Souter. When Jennens' and Bettridge's patent expired in 1839, making shell inlay for the japanners became a regular trade in Birmingham. Pieces of shell of contrasting iridescence were matched up so that one side of an inlay composition would show pink, the other green. Inlays of shell depicting historic buildings, such as Windsor Castle, or the Houses of Parliament by moonlight, were very popular. Flowers of tinted pearl, and large, acid-etched pearl plates of inlay became common after 1842. Although not all the little papier-mâché boxes and trays made in Birmingham received such full, elaborate treatment, some of them at least are good examples of the shell carver's art at its best.

*Chessboard with carved ivory and mother-of-pearl in-
lay by Jan Bellekin (1622). Courtesy Museum fur
Kunst und Gewerbe, Hamburg, Germany.*

Seventeenth century Dutch folk carving showing the fleets of Tarshish bringing gold, silver, ivory, apes, and peacocks to King Solomon. The legend is taken from I Kings, 10, 22. Courtesy Birmingham Museum, England.

Jewel box in mother-of-pearl inlay made by Charles Lyster, a Birmingham pearl and tortoiseshell worker living at Spencer Street, Birmingham, and presented by him to his daughter, Hannah Reading, on her wedding on June 18th, 1868. Courtesy Birmingham Museum, England.

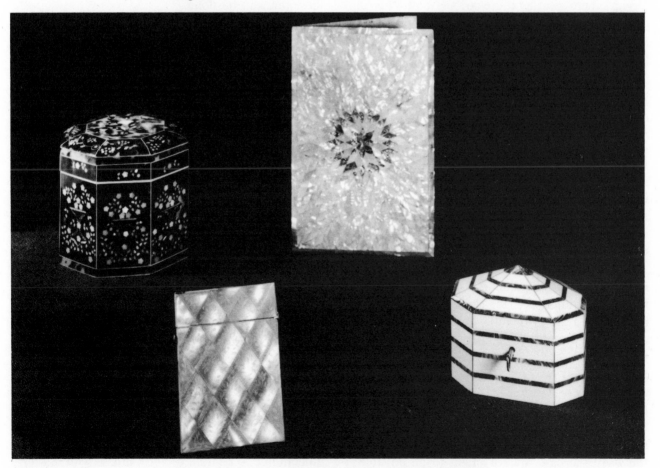

Tea caddies, book cover, and card case made by nineteenth-century Birmingham shell carver F. Stringer. Stringer worked in mother-of-pearl, tortoiseshell, ivory, and rosewood. Courtesy Birmingham Museum, England.

8

The Ship of Pearl:
The Nautilus Shell

In the warm waters of the Pacific and Indian Oceans there swarms a gregarious, bottom-feeding octopus called the pearly or chambered nautilus. Like someone who has shut up all his house except the basement, in which he lives, *nautilus pompilius* is content to live at the very mouth of his shell — and even this he shares with some sociable but parastic crustacea. The rest of the shell is "camerated" or sealed off into compartments of diminishing size, so that when the shell is cut open it reveals a section like a watch spring which has unwound. It is these sealed chambers which have made the nautilus a special shell from the carver's point of view; first of all they reduce the holding capacity of the shell, so as to make it a suitable size for a wine goblet — one nautilus which I have just picked out at random contains just over three-quarters of a pint — but more important, by building up a Daedalus-like maze in the interior of the shell, they provided the artist with a series of little boxes which he could open to the eye of the beholder. No doubt people of the sixteenth and seventeenth centuries were just as puzzled as we are by the function of these chambers, which are filled with nitrogen gas and have a direct connection between one another and the octopus. They are supposed to enable the nautilus to move up and down in the water, but if this were the case, then it ought to be possible to make a balloon ascend and descend by the same

principle, and so far no one has offered to show how this can be done.

When Vasco da Gama sailed into nautilus-filled waters for the first time, in 1498, he must have seen the inhabitants of the Nicobar coast making provision for the future by drying nautili for food. It was caught all over the Pacific and Indian oceans in basket traps baited with boiled crayfish, and nowhere was it caught in larger numbers than off Amboyna, which in 1609 became one of the corner stones of the Dutch East India Trading Company.

Even before Dutch seamen had a chance to walk along the tideless shore of the islands and see broken nautilus shells lying on the beach, showing their chambered structure and, under the handsome yellow-and-orange flared outer covering, the shimmering iridescent layer of nacre, they must have had a chance to admire Chinese carvings in the shell, such as the beautiful example preserved in the Fitzwilliam Museum, which appears to be a Ming dynasty carving roughly contemporary with its mount, which was made by a London goldsmith in 1585.

Although this is lightly engraved in the technique which is, rather regrettably, known in the West as "scratch carving," that is, blind engraving without any darkening of the lines — a treatment which was to continue to be used by the Chinese with masterly effect until the nineteenth century — they can lay

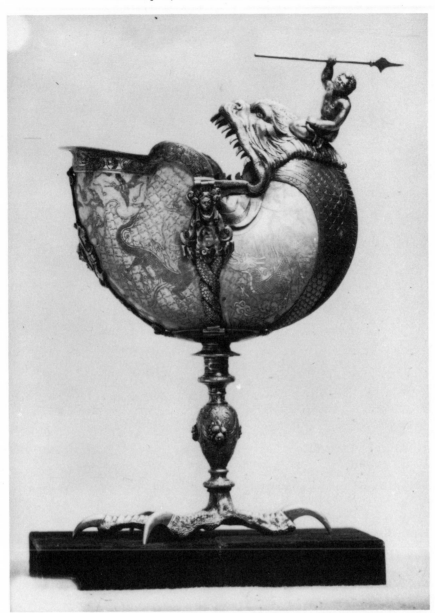

Long before nautilus carving had begun in Europe, the Chinese had begun both to cameo the shell and engrave it. This Chinese nautilus of the Ming dynasty, mounted in sixteenth-century German goldsmith's work, was the sort of object from which seventeenth-century Dutch carvers might have derived their inspiration. Courtesy British Museum, London.

claim to having invented another and much more widely employed scheme of nautilus decoration.

This is referred to in Ulyssus Aldrovandus' book *De Animalibus Exsanguinibus* as: "the nautilus from the Indies, ornamented with different figures carved in the outer rind." This method of carving, whereby part of the outer layer of the shell was "peeled" to produce a design in relief against the iridescent layer of nacre, a design heightened by relief sculpting and engraving on the nacreous layer itself, is well illustrated by another Ming dynasty shell, also in a sixteenth century, but this time Continental,

Stripped and polished nautilus shell set as a cup in Renaissance goldsmith's work of the sixteenth century. The flaring lip of the shell has been cut back to make a more convenient drinking vessel. Sixteenth-century German setting. Courtesy Waddesdon Collection British Museum, London.

mounting in the Waddesdon Collection in the British Museum. It bears a design of dragons whose bodies have been produced by sculpting away, as for a cameo, the brown and white outer layer. There is no reason to suppose that the Chinese craftsmen used any but their traditional tools, rubbing stone and knife and graver, to remove the outside layer, so that the Dutch techniques of revealing the pearl shell in a nautilus by using acids and mordants, which will be described in a moment, were an entirely original departure from traditional methods of dealing with the shell so far.

To the Dutch collectors of the seventeenth century, the nautilus, which they affectionately called "the little shipper," with its boat shape and its precious cargo of nacre, must have symbolized the *fluyts* which had brought the wealth of the Spice Islands to Holland. So identified indeed did the nautilus become with a ship that the opening of the shell is usually referred to as "the boat" by these writers of the seventeenth century who describe it.

It was fortunate for the nautilus-loving Dutch that they had, in the engravers of plaques for gun stocks who worked in the arms industries of Maestricht and Amsterdam, craftsmen who were trained in techniques which could easily be transferred to the pearl shell of the nautilus. Makers of ornaments for the butts of gun muskets and pistols had long been accustomed to cut-out inlays of stag horn, ivory, and mother-of-pearl which were ornamented by black line engravings before being let into the wooden stocks. One of these *monteurs d'arquebuses*, Jérémie Belquin, had moved his business of "master gun mounter and engraver of muskets" from Metz to Amsterdam, where both the political and religious atmosphere were more suitable for him. There he began to carve, not just plaques but shells as well, and he was succeeded by his son, Jean Bellequin, who was born in 1597 or thereabouts, and by his grandson, Cornelis Bellekin, who was to carry on the tradition of master shell carving into the eighteenth century. The Belkeins were the only nautilus shell carvers who signed their work, though other *Parelmoergraveurs* who are known to have been active in the seventeenth century, such as Jochem Kulme, Roeners, and Evans, may have

accounted for some of the unsigned nautili.

The methods of decoration and the techniques for ornamenting the shells evolved by the Belkeins and their concurrents were often combined in more than one nautilus, but they can, in essence, be reduced to six:

1. *The shell burnished but left plain.*

As this does not involve any carving, it need not be discussed here except that it was an indispensable prerequisite for engraving the mother-of-pearl layer. Rumphius describes the technique in his *Cabinet of Rareties from Amboyna (Amboinsche Rariteitkamer)* in 1705. The whole shell should be laid in some kind of acid for ten to twelve days, for instance in fermented rice, vinegar, or water in which some vine leaves have rotted. Then the outer coating is scoured off, beginning with the part where it is thickest. The stripped shell is then polished with diluted alchohol (*Sterk water*) until the beautiful luster of the mother-of-pearl appears. Then it is given a final rinse in soapy water, which will clean it and remove the remains of the acid, which would otherwise corrode the mother-of-pearl.

Stripped and polished nautilus shells continued to be popular down to the eighteenth century. The Victoria and Albert Museum possesses one fine example set in Polish goldsmith's work of about 1770 and ornamented with many intaglios. No doubt the basic shell had been processed in the East Indies just as Rumphius describes before being imported,

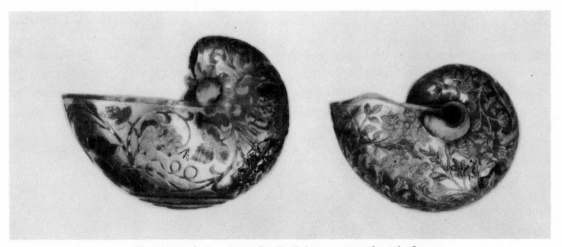

Two nautili by Cornelis Bellekin cameoed with flower designs cut in the outside of the shell. On one shell, left, insects have been engraved here and there in black line. Courtesy Rijksmuseum, Amsterdam, Holland.

Detail of nautilus by Cornelis Bellekin showing how the outer skin was removed in places so as to leave a design resembling openwork embroidery. Bergen. Courtesy Vestlandske Kunstindustri Museum, Holland.

After a short time the alcohol corrodes all the places in the shell where there is no wax, and the parts protected by wax remain raised up, so that in this way it can be decorated with all kinds of pictures and reliefs, which lie on top like loose work. And if there are some little corners which remain uneven they should be chiseled off with a little engraving iron, such as one uses to cut signets."

Swammerdam's reference to "loose work" inevitably suggests some kind of textile cut-out pattern or embroidery, and indeed the foliage designs so freely employed on these cameo nautili are perhaps connected with embroidery. At least a man's cap of about 1600 preserved in the Castle Museum, Nottingham, shows designs rather similar to that of many of the shells ornamented in this way.

probably through the great shell depot at Macassar.
2. *The outer crust of the shell cut into open work patterns, cameo fashion, so as to display a contrast between it and the iridescent layer of mother-of-pearl below.*

The method of producing these reliefs is described by Swammerdam in his Biblia *Naturae* in 1737. "First one takes yellow wax, thinning down with a little Venetian turpentine, to make it more fluid, and then one mixes in so much blackening that the color is strong enough. When the mixture has been melted in a spoon it can be used to paint the shell which it is desired to carve, and the places which were not covered with wax have to be painted with alcohol. This can easily be done with a little wooden pin to which a tiny piece of cloth has been tied.

Side of nautilus by Cornelis Bellekin showing openwork design cut from the outer layer. Bergen. Courtesy Vestlandske Kunstindustri Museum, Holland.

Swammerdam goes on to say that the alcohol should be thinned down with rain water for fear it corrodes the shell too much, and he discourages the use of other acids, such as nitric acid, on the shell, because they leave a chalky deposit.

Once the pattern was thus outlined in relief, the veins of the leaves and the petals of the flowers could be defined and incised with a graver. The whole pattern could have been cut out in this way, as was done by the Chinese, but of course it would have taken longer. One of the nautili which Sir Hans Sloane collected while on the Continent shows traces of black pigment (which may be the protective coating described) on the raised parts of

Nautilus by Cornelis Bellekin mounted in silver as a wine cup. Three of the main types of decoration of nautili have been employed on this shell. It has been engraved and the lines have been darkened. Openwork patterns have been cut on the outside of the shell and the chambers of the shell have been opened out and carved into an elaborate heraldic eagle and knight's helmet. Courtesy Vestlandske Kunstindustri Museum, Holland.

Back view of the Bergen shell by Cornelis Bellekin. The stripes which originally covered the whole of the outside of the untreated nautilus shell with a zebra pattern of brown and cream can be clearly seen. Bergen. Courtesy Vestlandske Kunstindustri Museum, Holland.

the shell. Marks on the mother-of-pearl spaces in the decoration also show that they were trimmed up by a square-ended graver being moved toward the line of raised decoration at right angles. Besides the Sloane shell there is a very fine nautilus with raised decoration in the Manchester Museum. Its rather obscure position is a dark display case in the Aquarium Section certainly does not enhance its aesthetic effect. The fact that it has never been published probably explains why it was apparently unknown to Van Seters when he wrote his great work on the nautilus, and he figures, as an example of this kind of decoration, a charming work

This view of the Cornelis Bellekin nautilus (from the left side) gives graphic expression to what the nautilus shell symbolized for Dutchmen of the seventeenth century—the riches of the gorgeous East, pouring into Holland's lap. In fact, the crew of this strange craft may represent the four continents. The two standing figures with feather bonnets are Red Indians, the rower is an African, the seated passenger with the monkey an Asiatic (probably a Turk), while Europe is indicated by the trumpeter proclaiming Holland's achievements and the very mondaine-looking lady with the fan. Courtesy Wadsworth Atheneum, Hartford, Connecticut.

Nautilus goblet attributed to Cornelis Bellekin. It seems unlikely that a superb draftsman such as Bellekin could have created the overstuffed elephant and disproportionate building which appear here. (View facing right.) Courtesy Wadsworth Atheneum, Hartford, Connecticut.

by Cornelis Bellekin in the Rijksmuseum, covered with a design of ripening vines, with the two bosses of the shell worked into harvest mice.

3. *The shell ornamented by pierced work, with decorative openings cut into the walls of the chambers.*

This method of decoration is alluded to by Rumphius, who says, "The clean [ie. stripped] shells are cut through where the little chambers are, so that the four or five last ones are open to the air. The three or four next chambers are cut out entirely and in the inner curl one cuts an opened little helmet." Rumphius goes on to describe how a crest and helmet cloth can be added to the visored helmet. He does not tell his readers how the cutting was done, but presumably it was with a twist drill and needle files. The wall of the nautilus shell is

*Engraved and carved nautilus shell by Cornelis Belle-
kin: Feast of Bacchus. Courtesy Musée du Louvre,
Paris.*

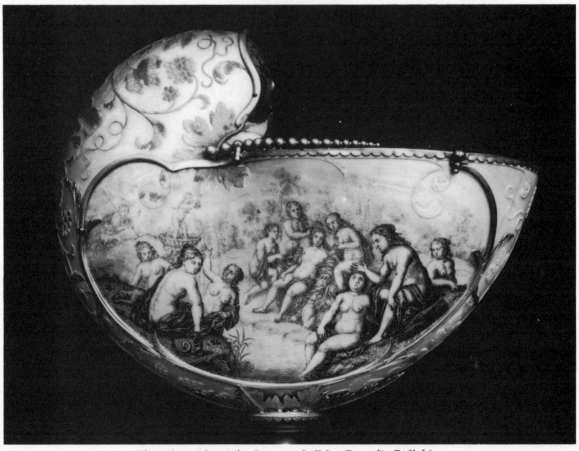

*The other side of the Louvre shell by Cornelis Bellekin.
This depicts Diana espied by Actaeon. Courtesy Musée
du Louvre, Paris.*

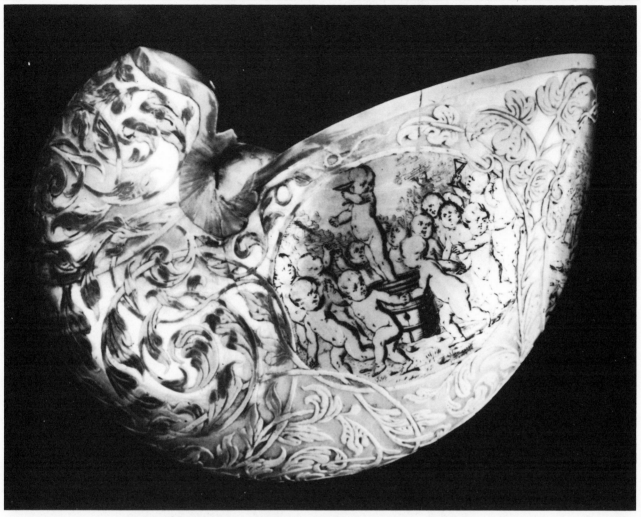

Cameoed and engraved nautilus of cupids. Courtesy
Sir Hans Sloane Collection, British Museum, London.

paper thin.

Not many nautili decorated in this way would appear to have survived. There is one, ornamented with a crested helm, in the Sloane Collection, but I can only recall seeing one with openings in the side chambers, a very good example in Manchester, probably much better than anything Van Seters had seen. The antiquity of this kind of decoration however, is emphasized by a sixteenth-century drawing of a nautilus with opened wall, while several seventeenth-century paintings by Johann Georg Hainz, W. Kalff, and Jan David de Heem (the last of which is in the Wallace Collection) testify to its popularity.

I myself find it difficult to understand the popularity of the helmet form of decoration. It was a theme which must have been very limiting to the artist — though of course it would enable the owner of a nautilus to identify himself with his possession if he had his own crest placed above the helmet. On the other hand it is perfectly easy to appreciate the fascination with which people of the time would regard the unsealed chambers of the nautilus, and admire the shimmering iridescence, which, as one old naturalist puts it, "no mortal eye was intended to enjoy."

Wrecked is the ship of pearl
 And every chambered cell
Where its dim dreaming life was wont to dwell
As the frail tenant shaped his growing shell
Before thee lies revealed
Its irised ceiling rent, its sunless crypt unsealed.

Nautilus set as a cup by Cornelis Bellekin. W. H. Van Seters suggested that the themes of the two sides of this shell depict, respectively, "Woman" and "Man." The author's feeling is that they are "Peace" and "War." The knob in the fold of the nautilus has been sculpted into a woman's head on the "Peace" side and into the head of a soldier wearing a military moustache on the other. Courtesy Wadsworth Atheneum, Hartford, Connecticut.

Of course the very method of decoration employed, which weakened the structure of the shell so much that if it were once dropped, it would be irretrievably damaged, would explain the infrequency with which it can be seen in collections.

4. *Shells decorated with blind engravings.*

I have only seen one of these, in Manchester. It has been engraved with a veiner, but no pigment has been put into the lines, in the Chinese manner. The subject of the decoration is seventeenth-century European, however, and the omission of the pigment is obviously a matter of deliberate choice.

5. *Shells engraved with black line engravings.*

"On the sides around the little boat that is, the

On this anonymous Dutch nautilus shell of the seventeenth century, three schemes of decoration have been carried out. Part of the outer shell has been left as a border, which is partly plain, partly cut into scalloped designs. The heads of the figures have, daringly and successfully, been carved in low relief. This is nearly an impossible task considering how thin the nautilus is, even here at the inner corner of the shell, where it is thickest. Figures and ships have been engraved with a skill which suggests the professional engraver. The designs depict naval triumphs of Holland. Here is Van Tromp as Neptune, clutching a seventeenth-century ship's rudder. Courtesy British Museum, London.

The other side of the Van Tromp shell at the British Museum. It depicts Jan Eversten, Vice Admiral of Zeeland (d. 1666). Courtesy British Museum, London.

mouth of the shell," Rumphius comments, "one can cut all kinds of figures which can then be darkened with powdered coal, mixed with wax or oil, till they show up black." Sometimes an engraving of this sort would be set in a frame made from relief work such as has been described earlier.

The engraved lines were of course cut with the same tool which cut lines in a copper plate for printing, a mushroom-handled graver. The handle was held in the palm of the hand and the point pushed away from the engraver.

Engraved nautilus shells are probably the most common form of ornamented shells to survive; they are represented by whole shells, as at Manchester, and also in the form of broken shells, such as the magnificent marine triumph of De Ruyter and Van Tromp in the Sloane Collection, or fragments like

that in the Ashmolean.

6. *Direct relief sculpture.*

There was very little scope for this in the restricted thickness of the shell. Carving relief in a nautilus was rather like trying to cut one in the thickness of a piece of wallpaper. Some artists managed to do this, however, probably in order to demonstrate a *tour de maitre*. The heads of the two naval heroes in the Sloane marine triumph are both relief carved, their bodies being engraved. It is much more usual, however, for relief carving to be applied to some outstanding knob or boss on the shell, which is often cleverly turned into a face, or a harvest mouse, by one of the Belkeins.

The subject matter of decoration followed that of contemporary work in mother-of-pearl. Openwork decoration necessarily had to be confined to comparatively simple themes such as garlands and foliage; pierced work was limited to a few appealing types of decorative openings, but in engraving the artist's fancy could wander much further afield.

Mythological themes are popular both with Jan Belkein and his successors. There is a good example of infant bacchantes on a nautilus by Jan in the Sloane Collection. The same artist delighted in "Farmer's Joys," scenes of rustic merrymaking, often further enriched by delicately drawn flying insects on the part of the shell not occupied by the main picture, such as in the example in the Fredriks Collection in The Hague.

Cornelis was faithful to the tradition but enriched it. He chose scenes of country amusements, such as the example from the Hofmuseum in Vienna, but

also had a strong penchant for themes such as the Rape of Europa, and the Venus and Juno in the Van Aalst collection at Hoevelaken. His contemporary scenes, such as those in "Man and Woman" in the Pierpoint Morgan Collection at Hartford, Connecticut, are perhaps his most successful undertakings.

Cornelis seems to have composed his own pictures, though other members of the family such as Jan Belkein, occasionally employed the prints of other artists, such as Pieter Quaast.

To descend from the conscious artistry and freedom of Cornelis Bellekin to the arid years of the later eighteenth and early nineteenth centuries is to pass from plenty to want. Engravers like Barckhuysen, who were led by the prints of contemporary

Anonymous seventeenth-century Dutch nautilus shell. The chambers have been opened in an elaborate design and it has been engraved in blackened line. The flairing lip of the nautilus has been cut down. The design shows the fall of Phaeton. Courtesy Manchester Museum, England.

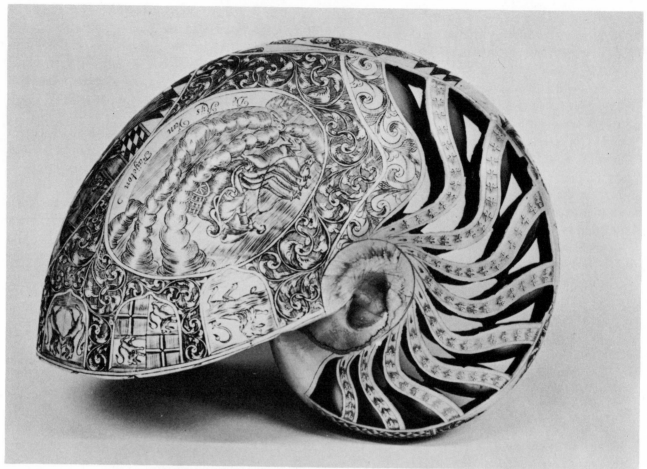

The other side of the Phaeton nautilus. Note the heraldic shields which ring the lip, and the naive and rather crude draftsmanship. Courtesy Manchester Museum, England.

engravers, and whose gravers were lacking in the airy lightness of the Belkein family, saw the century out.

By Victorian times, nautilus engravings was merely a curiosity, and perhaps it was with the intention of surprising the visitors to the Great Exhibition of 1851 in London that a humble working man named Wood entered his exhibit. The *Morning Chronicle* of 22nd May, 1851, described it as follows:

A curious specimen of patient industry, sent in by a working man . . . is to be seen in the Fine Arts Court, by the side of the model of the statue of the late George Bentinck. It is an engraved nautilus shell —the only instrument employed being a small penknife. The shell is dedicated to the memory of Nelson. Upon the front is represented the globe, with Britannia seated upon the Lion, and possessed of the usual emblems of sovereignty, surrounded with a border composed of oak leaves and acorns, most elaborately engraved. Upon each side are a number of lines from Fitzgerald, commemorative of the victories of Nelson—so small, however, that they almost require the aid of a microscope to decipher them. Upon one side of the shell is a representation of Peace, seated on the prow of the vessel, pointing to the victories achieved by the hero, and upon the other is represented George and the Dragon; the head of the shell represents that of a parrot. The designs are most artistic and the execution remarkably fine.

Shortly before the exhibition, Wood presented to Queen Victoria: "a similar shell, on which was engraved, with the same rude graver, the royal arms, the Prince of Wales' feathers, the *Great Britain* and the *Great Western* steamships with a full description of the same, also several verses from Pope, amounting altogether to about 1,500 words, which were

The back of the Phaeton shell, with a court jester and another scene from court life. Courtesy Manchester Museum, England.

Anonymous seventeenth-century Dutch nautilus. Like some other shells, the heavy nature of the drawing suggests the craftsman rather than the engraver. This is a unique shell because the engraving is "undarkened," like that of Chinese scratch carving. Was this because the carver engraved it and had it taken from his hands by an impatient patron before he could rub it with coal dust? Perhaps some owner of the shell washed it too vigorously. Courtesy Manchester Museum, England.

tastefully engraved in German text, Old English, Roman, and Italic characters." The Queen ordered that Wood should be given a sum of money, and a few days later sent him a proof impression of Sir G. Hayter's print of her coronation, "framed, and tastefully ornamented with the rose, shamrock, and thistle in burnished and dead gold."

"This circumstance" the *Morning Chronicle,* concludes "while it attests the ability of the poor man, affords also an interesting proof of her Majesty's kindness and condescension in recognizing the merits of a humble mechanic."

By great luck I stumbled upon the only remaining works of Wood in the vaults of the National Maritime Museum, Greenwich, London, England, while researching a previous book, *Modern Ivory*

Carving. They consist of two shells, one of which is, in Wood's own words, "a counterpart of the one exhibited in class 30, Great Exhibition, 1851." This is of course the shell representing the victories of Nelson. Unfortunately it is badly broken. The other shell is also a copy, this time of the shell showing the *Great Britain* and *Great Western.* The carver has inscribed on it, "This shell is Engraved with a common Penknife, and similar to the one presented to H. M. Gracious Majesty, Queen Victoria, By C. H. Wood, 1845."

Evidently Wood liked repeating his successes. He also made use of his designs more than once, even on shells which were not intended to be copies, one of another. Thus the design for "Peace" has been used on both shells. The head of the interior

C. H. Wood is the signature on the Great Eastern
nautilus. The legend states, "This shell is Engraved
with a common Penknife: and similar to the one presented to H. M. Gracious Majesty Queen Victoria."
Courtesy National Maritime Museum, Greenwich,
England.

C. Wood, the only British nautilus shell carver to be
recorded, seems to have eked out a scanty livelihood
by presenting shells to patrons, and then being recom-
pensed by them. Here is one which he presented to
W. L. Prior. Courtesy National Maritime Museum,
Greenwich, England.

One side of this nautilus by C. H. Wood is engraved with the Great Eastern *and* Great Britain *steamships, 1845. This is a facsimile of one presented to Queen Victoria. Courtesy National Maritime Museum, Greenwich, England.*

Another view of the Great Eastern *and* Great Britain. *Courtesy National Maritime Museum, Greenwich, England.*

of the shell is also turned into a goat in both. Wood's engraving is made up of scores which are roughly triangular-shaped in section. Probably he used the point of the penknife to scrape some lines sideways. Other cuts have a serrated edge as though made by a series of tiny digs or jabs. Wood uses the same leaf ornament which appears in American and British scrimshaw, and it would be interesting to know if he had ever had any connection with the sea. Certainly the nautilus shells which he carved were pieces of glorified scrimshaw. Wood dedicates one of them to a patron. No doubt the fact that he was, as he is careful to note, "Patronized by Her Majesty the Queen," brought him numerous orders. Although no great draughtsman, and much less happy with faces than ships, Wood's work deserves notice, not merely because he is a genuine working-class artist, but because he was the very last carver of nautilus shell worthy of attention.

9

The Sounding Shell:
Tortoiseshell in Europe

THERE IS NO SUCH THING AS TORTOISESHELL. WHAT we know by that name are the plates from the carapaces of three species of large marine turtles. This was not always the case; at one time the tortoiseshell did include shell from some tortoises. "Of the shells of the smaller land-tortoises not much use is now commercially made," wrote an English author in 1879. "And they find no sale in this country. They were formerly worked up in the manufacture of ornamental articles, such as tea-caddies, work boxes, card-cases, side-combs, etc; but they have fallen almost into disuse, being superseded by the marine tortoise-shell. In the Cape Colony [South Africa] the dorsal shield or shell of a small land-tortoise, about three inches in diameter, which is very beautiful, is made into a snuff-box. This kind is used, more especially on the Continent, in buhl furniture, and occasionally in England for inlaying tables, cabinets, picture-frames, and other ornamental articles; a suitable foil being placed below it, to give lustre and colour." Enough tortoiseshell has probably been obtained from tortoises in the past to justify retaining the name — *turtleshell,* a term used by some scientific writers, is zoologically correct, but exceptionable because of its lack of associations and because it is always a nuisance to have two names for the same material.

Tortoiseshell is one of the most widely distributed of all art materials. During the nineteenth century it was shipped to America from India and China, the East Indies, the Pacific Islands, Australia, the West Indies, South America, and Africa. Most of this shell was shipped via London, which acted as the receiving center for the trade; during the seventies of last century between twenty-five and thirty tons of shell were imported to England every year. At this time, tortoiseshell was worth 14/6d. a pound, except for Indian tortoiseshell, which was valued at only half as much. Prices fluctuated a good deal, because the principal use for tortoiseshell has always been for making combs. So the demand for the shell varied according to contemporary fashions in hairdressing. In countries such as Spain, the former Spanish colonies, and the Far East, where fashions changed more slowly, the demand for tortoiseshell was constant. One of the principal manufactures in the shell in the United States, for example was back combs for the Spanish peninsula and the South American markets. "They were often a couple of feet wide, encircling two-thirds of the head, and from six inches to a foot high on the back, the top being wrought in open work; to these the Spanish ladies attached their veils. As much of the work was done by hand and with the saw, and the polishing was entirely manual, the prices were high."

The shell used in the manufacture of tortoiseshell came from three turtles: the hawksbill, loggerhead, and green turtle. The last of these deserves to be mentioned first, because it was probably the first to be discovered, owing to its delicious flavor. The

162

Tortoiseshell snuffbox by John Obrisset with pressed tortoiseshell portrait of Queen Anne. Courtesy British Museum, England.

green turtle (*chelone mydas*) is one of the most historic of all dishes. Long before the Roman Empire had arisen, whole tribes around the Red Sea lived on little else. Diodorus of Sicily, Pliny, and Strabo mention its eating qualities. The heyday for turtle-eating began in the seventeenth century, when the buccaneers began to settle in the West Indies. They used an old Carib Indian recipe, cooking the turtle over a hole filled with red hot charcoal. Overnight, one of the great dishes of the world was born. Father Lobat, a seventeenth-century French monk and travel writer, gave his readers the perfect recipe:

> The plastron or buckler is the shell of the belly, on which is left three or four inches of flesh, with all the fat, this being green, and of a very delicate flavor. The plastron is placed in the oven. It is seasoned with lemon juice, capsicum or cayenne, salt, pepper, cloves, and eggs beaten up. The oven ought not to be too hot, as the flesh of the turtle being tender it should be cooked slowly. While it is baking the flesh must be pierced from time to time with a wooden skewer, so that the gravy may penetrate all parts. The shell is sent up to table, and the meat carved out from it. I have never eaten anything more appetizing or better flavored.

In the English West Indies, too, there were special recipes for turtle soup. "The soup made there is flavored with sherry, and seasoned with strong spices, capsicum, ginger, cloves, and nutmeg. It is considered to be excellent, when, after having eaten,

one is obliged to rest with the mouth open, and cool the fevered palate with madeira or port. So that to appreciate this fiery soup, the taste has to be acquired."

During the eighteenth century, turtle became a passion to the citizens of London. The arrival of fresh turtles was announced in the *Gentleman's Magazine*, and no banquet at the Guildhall, where the London Livery Companies of Guildsmen met, or at the Mansion House, where the Lord Mayor of London entertained the Aldermen who had elected him, was considered complete unless turtle soup was on the menu. Special inns, such as the *Ship and Turtle*, and *Birch's* throve on the preparation of turtle dishes.

Tortoiseshell carving, and the peculiar plastic properties of the shell, about which more will be said later, were almost certainly discovered by someone who had just eaten a turtle. The flakes of tortoiseshell on the carapace, which look so dull and lifeless in their natural state — even when the reptile is alive and swimming close to the surface of the water — become beautifully glowing and

Tortoiseshell snuffbox by John Obrisset. Note same pressed tortoiseshell portrait of Queen Anne as in previous picture. Courtesy British Museum, London.

transparent the moment they are wiped with something greasy, such as fingers smeared with turtle fat for example. Furthermore, tortoiseshell can be softened and molded by the heat of the fire, or by boiling in salt water, processes to which shell would be subjected while it was being cooked, either on an open fire, or *boucan,* as described above, or in the large cauldrons used by Greek and Roman sailors for cooking food on the seashore. It is no coincidence that the first reports of shell being used for craft purposes come from areas where the green turtle was widely eaten, around the Red Sea.

In spite of its edible qualities, the green turtle does not provide good shell. Its plates are thin and flexible. Their color is a dull palish brown, streaked with patches of black, but with none of the mottling which distinguishes the Hawksbill's shell. The shell of the green turtle resembles horn more than any other turtle shell. Besides its color, which shows up with greenish reflections, the shell is difficult to weld. It is a second-best shell at the best, but has been widely used at one time or another for veneering. The poor quality of the green turtle's shell may come from its diet; it feeds on delicate marine algae. The habits of this turtle, and of the others which are described later, make it an easy prey to fishermen. It can be caught swimming in the open sea and

Tortoiseshell snuffbox by John Obrisset with lid portrait of Prince George of Denmark. Courtesy British Museum, London.

harpooned, or overturned, or caught in staked nets. most turtles, however, are secured as they crawl ashore to lay their eggs. A female turtle may lay as many as 250 eggs at a time. The beaches where turtles lay are well known and watched during the laying season. Green turtles can attain a considerable size, nearly four feet long, and weigh more than 336 pounds. Apart from the size of the shell, the age of a turtle can be guessed by the number of rings inside the hexagonal plates on the back. Shell craftsmen always added more salt to the water when boiling and softening shell from an older turtle. They could tell the age of all the shell they used because all the plates on a carapace were strung together, through a small hole bored in each plate, and sold as a whole.

The loggerhead turtle or caret turtle (*thalassochelys caretta*) included the Mediterranean as well as the intertropical seas in its range. Many loggerheads were caught in the Pacific and they provided a good deal of the shell used in the Far East. The scales of the loggerhead are a dark chestnut brown, thin, and neither clear nor beautifully colored. The loggerhead lived on shells, mollusks, crustaceans, and fish, and was not used for food.

The turtle *par excellence* is the hawksbill (*Chelone imbricata*). Although it is a small turtle, and a new-

Tortoiseshell snuffbox by John Obrisset with a portrait of Queen Anne. Courtesy British Museum, London.

Seventeenth- or eighteenth-century snuffbox with piqué *designs in* cloué. *Courtesy Victoria and Albert Museum, London.*

French piqué bonbonniére, *or sweetmeat box, in the style of Louis XV, dated about the middle of the eighteenth century. It is encrusted with diaper ornament and foliated scrolls in both* cloué *and* posé. *Courtesy Wallce Collection, London.*

ly caught specimen, newly landed on the waterfront at Las Palmas in the Canaries, seemed to me almost like a miniature of the larger turtles, it carries a lot of shell. A specimen of the maximum size, about three feet long, may yield up to eight pounds in tortoiseshell. The range of the hawksbill extends over all the tropical and subtropical seas. It used to be fished by inhabitants of the West Indian Islands, but the fishermen are now being lured away from a hazardous and insecure profession to more settled work in Florida. Besides producing thick plates, the carapace of the Hawksbill provides beautifully colored shell. The thirteen large plates on the back are of a translucent mottled amber, brown, and red. The belly of the turtle is covered with blonde plates, while the side pieces are a mixture of dark and blonde shell. Once netted, harpooned, and overturned on shore, the turtle

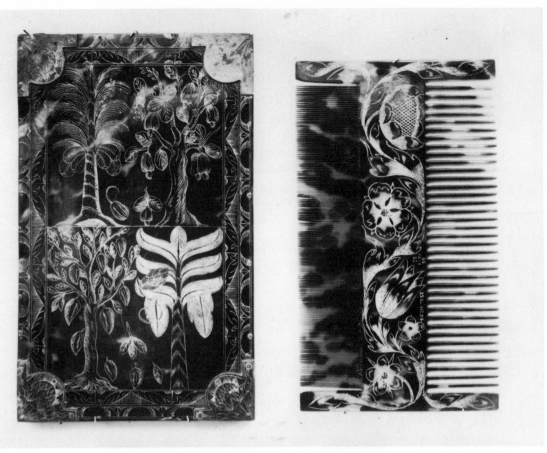

Tortoiseshell comb and case of perhaps the seventeenth century. From the Bern Collection. Courtesy British Museum, London.

Standish attributed to André Charles Boulle, side view. Courtesy Wallace Collection, London.

Standish (pen and-ink holder) attributed to André Charles Boulle (1642-1733). The date (1710) and the reference in the inscription running around the top of the standish to several important personages at Louis XIV's court, including Georges Marechel, the king's surgeon and councillor, indicate that this attribution is probably correct, as it emanates from the courtly clientele for whom Boulle worked. Courtesy Wallace Collection, London.

would have its carapace removed. The plates would adhere to this until taken off, and complete, polished carapaces are a fairly frequent sight. The plates of shell would be detached by heating, or by soaking the carapace in boiling water. In the West Indies they were removed by burying the carapace in the ground sand for ten or twelve days. It was the first task of the tortoiseshell craftsman to select such plates as had not been badly damaged by removal, through splitting because of too much heat, for example, or had been marred while the reptile was still alive through limpets attaching themselves to the shell.

There had been tortoiseshell long before there was any tortoiseshell carving. The discovery of the uses to which the shell could be put in art came as an afterthought, almost an accident. Unlike most of the great discoveries in art, it is associated with the name of just one discoverer: Carvillius Pollio.

Pollio, a well-to-do amateur living in Rome during the days of Nero, was a dilettante of genius, an exception to the average Roman citizen, who too often was a Philistine incapable of forming an artistic judgment for himself and blindly dependent on his professional connoisseur, a Greek slave. Pollio had already made history in interior decoration in Rome by designing gold and silver ornaments for the couches on which diners reclined around the meal table. He now investigated the properties of an exotic substance imported by the Romans from their Far Eastern trading Centers, and instructed the craftsmen under his direction to saw plates of tortoiseshell into veneers with which to decorate these and other pieces of furniture.

Of course tortoiseshell, as a material, had long been known to the Romans and other people in the Western world. The Assyrians had carved representations on their bas-reliefs of turtles swimming in the water beside Assyrian ships. The stilted manner in which the amphibians are depicted suggests that they may have only observed them on dry land. Scattered tribes on the periphery of the Roman Empire, dwellers along the shores of the Red Sea and the Indian Ocean, had long made turtle-fishing their principal livelihood. Their method of capture was original and simple. They found that turtles tended

to come to the surface during the forenoon, or at night, when they had visited the shore. Often they would doze on the surface, betraying their whereabouts (according to the Roman naturalist Pliny) by the noise of their snoring. The fisherman would slip noiselessly from their boats into the water, three of them attaching themselves to each turtle. Two of them would suddenly turn the sleeping amphibian upside down in the water, so that it floated helplessly on its back, while a third swimmer would throw a lasso around its neck. Watchers on the shore would haul in the line and draw the turtle to land.

The "tortoise-eaters," or *chelonophages* as they were called in Greek, lived on a rather indeterminate part of the coast between Egypt and the Persian Gulf. Strabo also talks about the Chelonophages of Arabia, as though there were a separate colony of them there. They were simple folk, with little use for any part of turtles except the insides. They

Eighteenth-century French tray in boulle. *It is decorated with a marquetry of white metal, tortoiseshell, and brass. Courtesy Victoria and Albert Museum, London.*

Stand attributed to André Charles Boulle. Courtesy Wallace Collection, London.

Door attributed to André Charles Boulle. Courtesy Wallace Collection, London.

did however, make armour of tortoiseshell scales, which they also used to roof their houses (a single carapace, says Pliny, would roof the family hut), and they even made skiffs from the carapaces of turtles, in which they were able to put to sea. This last piece of information suggests that turtles grew to a much larger size in antiquity, possibly even before the Industrial Revolution, than they do now. Certainly Dampier, the eighteenth-century buccaneer and explorer, saw a turtle shell, six feet across, being used as a skiff by a small boy. In the days when great fleets of turtles studded the waters of the eastern Mediterranean or poured into the mouth of

Front of a cabinet, probably from the workshop of André Charles Boulle. Courtesy Wallace Collection, London.

the river Eleutherus, there must have been many which grew to their full maturity and achieved monster size, especially as turtles are "extremely tenacious of life, capable of extraordinary abstinence, and of living long after having sustained injuries which would have been immediately destructive to almost any other animal. They are also remarkable for their longevity." Just such a monster turtle, four and a half feet across the shell, was sent as a present from an Indian king called Porus to Caesar Augustus. Other gifts included an armless man called Herman, large serpents ten ells long, a partridge bigger than a vulture, and a certain Zarmanochagus from Bargosa who showed his value as a curiosity by later burning himself alive in Athens, as Indians were wont to do, either when affairs were going very badly for them, so that they could escape present ills, or when life was prosperous, so that they might avoid the ill fortune that was bound to follow. From the description of these gifts, it sounds as though they may have been intended for a menagerie. There was evidently no thought that the turtle would be useful for tortoiseshell. In fact, the enormous qualities of shell produced apparently found no use except in medicine. The ancient Egyptians consented to receive turtle carapaces as tribute. When Julius Caesar captured Alexandria he found so many carapaces that he had them carried in his triumph. These may have been the carapaces, however, not of turtles, but of tortoises. By the time of the Greek occupation of Egypt, tortoiseshell had become a recognized object of commerce, though there is no record that it was ever used there for decorative purposes. It did, however, play a large part in contemporary medicine. Its flesh was claimed to be a cure for the bites of venomous insects and serpents, besides being a sort of universal panacea for all diseases. Even the smoke of burning meat was sufficient to drive off magical artifices and combat poisons. When, finally, we learn that scrapings of the shell were regarded as a most powerful aphrodisiac it is no longer necessary to wonder why there should be a traffic in it, even before it had been adapted for decorative purposes.

It was all the more surprising that no one before the Romans had employed tortoiseshell for artistic purposes, because Greek legend told how it had been first put to use to make musical instruments. The god Hermes had found the carapace of a tor-

*Cabinet attributed to André Charles Boulle. Courtesy
Wallace Collection, London.*

Back of a cabinet from the worksohp of André Charles Boulle. Courtesy Wallace Collection, London.

Mirror back in the manner of André Charles Boulle.
Courtesy Wallace Collection, London.

Nineteenth-century English tea caddies ornamented with piqué *and inlay in ivory and mother-of-pearl. Courtesy Victoria and Albert Museum, London.*

toise on Mount Chelydorea; he used it to construct the first lyre. Although later in Greek and Roman history lyres were made from materials other than tortoiseshell, the early ones were probably just the carapace of a tortoise. In later lyres the bottom of the instrument continued to be made from tortoiseshell. Here possibly lies another explanation of the discovery of tortoiseshell. Even if the shells from which lyres were made had not been polished, the friction of the hand of the lyrist on the surface of the carapace would have smoothed them somewhat, while the perspiration of the musician's hand or the unguents with which the ancients anointed themselves, would have eventually added a polish to the surface of the lyre. Possibly the carapace of a marine turtle was employed for a lyre soundbox, and the superior qualities of translucency and color of turtle shell were thus discovered.

However he hit upon it, Pollio's discovery that tortoiseshell could be adapted for ornamental purposes soon became the rage of aristocratic Rome. Patricians hastened to ornament their doors and the columns of their houses with sheets of shell veneer. Nor were the Romans content with just the natural colors of the shell. "During the reign of Nero," wrote Pliny, "by an unheard-of invention we have come to deprive tortoiseshell of its real appearance by means of dyes, and to make it more expensive by forming it into imitation of woods. Thus it is that couches are enhanced, thus it is that men want to out-do the craftsman who works in terebinth, to obtain a citron wood more precious than the real thing, and to imitate maple. Lately, wood was too common a material for luxury, now it has turned tortoiseshell into wood." So prized did furniture covered with tortoiseshell become among the Romans that "couches made from Indian tortoiseshell," are referred to by Roman legal textbooks as a likely legacy of value which might be disputed in the law-courts. The demand for tortoiseshell continued right through the latter centuries of the Roman Empire. Hippalus, a third-century A.D. Roman navigator, shortened the voyage to the tortoiseshell regions by discovering the regularity of the monsoon winds. A Roman book of directions for navigators, called The *Periplus [Sailing Round] of the Erythraean Sea* [the Indian Ocean], describes difficulties and dangers of the tortoiseshell trade. The people of the coast were little better than pirates, and were giants into the bargain. Much of the trade had to be carried on by means of Arab middlemen, who had married local women and spoke the language. They imported wheat, which they distributed to the people of the coast to gain their goodwill, and in return for the great quantities of tortoiseshell, ivory, and rhinoceros horn which

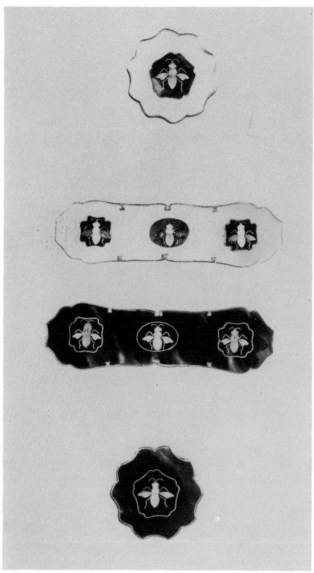

Nineteenth-century French boxes of counters, alternately in dark tortoiseshell and mother-of-pearl, inlaid with piqué. *The heraldic device of the bee suggests that they were owned by Emperor Napolean I, or some member of his family. This imperial design appears on many Napoleonic relics, which, incidentally, the Marquis of Hertford (founder of the Wallace Collection) was in a good position to buy in Paris after 1815. Courtesy Wallace Collection.*

they bought from them, the Arabs supplied lances, specially made at Muza for the trade, hatchets, daggers, awls and Alexandrian glass.

With the fall of the Roman Empire, tortoiseshell work abandoned the West — for a time. The art took refuge in the East. Tortoiseshell bracelets,

armlets, and other ornaments continued to be made until lately in Gujarat and Bombay, in India, in a way which probably represented centuries of traditional craftsmanship. From India, shell craftsmanship may have spread to Egypt, and it was no doubt from the latter country that the Neapolitan tortoiseshell workers, who were active at the end of the fifteenth century, learned their art.

In 1495 the army of Charles VIII of France marched into an unresisting Naples. On the French king's withdrawal from the city he took with him some tortoiseshell workers, who proceeded to introduce the art to France. Naples had not been denuded of tortoiseshell workers, however, and during the seventeenth century — the heyday of the tortoiseshell worker's art — a Neapolitan called Laurentini invented an entirely new process of ornamenting shell called *piqué*.

Several factors had produced a renaissance of tortoiseshell art in Europe. Samuel Pitiscus, the great Dutch classical scholar, writing at the age of seventy-five in 1713, commented ruefully that the Romans had produced splendid tortoiseshell veneers, but that nothing of that kind was to be seen in contemporary Holland. Travelers to the East, however, brought back reports that the same kind of work was still being made there, only he had not seen it. Even while Pitiscus wrote, tortoiseshell working had been introduced to France, and had invaded England. Many of the patrons of the new craft must have been collectors who owned, or had inspected, Far Eastern tortoiseshell work and wanted something of the same sort made for them at home. Supplies of tortoiseshell were becoming sufficiently large to meet the new demand owing to the setting up of new trading companies sailing to Africa and the Far East. The need for tortoiseshell was not lost on these new trading ventures. A ship taking French merchants and the explorer Chambonneau to Senegal even had to allow the crew to attempt to capture a turtle seen swimming in the sea. There was a very long tradition of horn working in many parts of Europe, and most of the processes used in horn-work could be applied with equal success to tortoiseshell. If tortoiseshell had to be carved it could be sculpted with the same tools which an ivory carver used. Accordingly it is not surprising to find that one of the principal centers for tortoiseshell work developed in a town which had already a splendid tradition in ivory carving and in horn work, Dieppe.

Dieppe carving had begun some time in the sixteenth century when the entrepreneur Jean Angot brought in workmen from other parts of Europe. During the seventeenth and eighteenth centuries, Dieppe had become a center for the supply of ecclesiastical articles, such as crucifixes, and for all kinds of luxury wares. The work methods of the Dieppe carver had become fixed by the nineteenth century and no doubt they did not vary much from those employed in earlier centuries. The artist worked in a very small, cramped workshop of his own, or alongside other workers in a larger *atelier*. The workshops were filled with the raw material of the trade: tusks, bones, horns, and shell. Before the carver began work he would choose a design from among those which he had drawn for him

German bass viol of the early eighteenth century, probably made by Joachim Tielke. There is an elaborate tortoiseshell and ivory design on the fingerboard. Courtesy Victoria and Albert Museum, London.

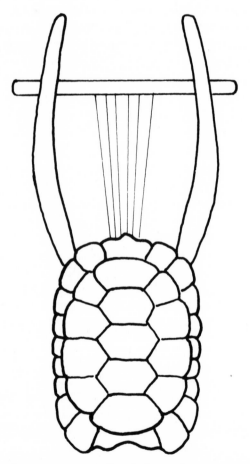

Lyre of sycamore wood and the entire carapace of a tortoise, from Athens, fifth century B.C. Courtesy British Museum, London.

self, cut from printed books, or had drawn for him by his master, if he were an apprentice. These would be pasted into a pattern book which he would keep on the bench in front of him. The carver would rarely have enjoyed any instruction in art, but he would be full of the innate skill of the Normans and have a burning desire to become a good carver. Without such a desire he would hardly have submitted himself to a long apprenticeship followed by a lifetime of rather scanty reward for his work. Not infrequently he would be a hereditary carver whose family had been known in the town for many years. Often he would be a Protestant, which was important, because Louis XIV offered the French Hu-

Bass viol made by Martin Voigt of Hamburg, in 1726, inlaid with mother-of-pearl and ebony. Courtesy Victoria and Albert Museum, London.

guenots the choice between forced conversion or banishment, many of them preferred to leave France forever, taking their precious trade secrets with them. The bench at which the carver worked was a peculiar one, it looked like a dining table with a very large circular recess cut out of it, so as to let a fat diner sit further in. The bench was called an *établi,* the semi-circular recess a *grelle.* In the middle of the recess protruded a sawing pin called a *taquet* — a sailor's term which reminds us what strong connections Dieppe art had with the sea. The carver held whatever he was carving in an ingenious hand-vice called a *main* with one hand, while he worked away with the tool, using his other hand. The Dieppe artists used a variety of specially designed tools, bone saws, chisels, burins, gouges, and a sort of saw file with deeply cut steps called a *grêle* or *écouane.* The latter tool looked very much like the tools used by contemporary African ivory carvers in Malawi, in Central Africa. They seem clumsy, but are extremely effective in the right hands. The most useful tool for work in tortoiseshell was probably the bow drill. This was an implement virtually identical with that from the South Sea Islands. It could be used for drilling holes which were to be enlarged with a piercing saw. Much of the orna-

Bass viol by Martin Voigt of Hamburg, in 1726, with
marquetry designs in tortoiseshell, ebony, and ivory.
Another view of Martin Voigt's bass viol of 1726.
Courtesy Victoria and Albert Museum, London.

Baryton by Jacques Sainprae, Berlin, 1720. Tortoise-shell and ivory marquetry on the fingerboard and tail-piece. Courtesy Victoria and Albert Museum, London.

German Baryton by Jacques Sainprae, Berlin, 1720, with tortoiseshell and ivory marquetry on the finger-board and tailpiece. (Detail of last picture.) Courtesy Victoria and Albert Museum, London.

mentation of seventeenth-century musical instru-ment which were inlaid with tortoiseshell took the form of elaborately shaped pieces of inlay, which would required to be pierced in a score of places if it were to be cut out safely. The Dieppe carvers had also developed the use of the bow drill, not merely for making holes for saw cuts, but for carry-ing out any kind of fretwork or pierced patterns. The workman would begin by drilling one hole in a piece of fretted ornament, then make another slightly to one side of it, a third in a straight line on the opposite side of the first, and so on, until he had made a quincunx, or cross, of little holes. The use of the bow drill probably contributed to the development of *piqué*. This consists of a design of minute gold or silver nails which are forced into

the surface of a tortoiseshell box. These nails could be forced into the shell while it was hot and pliant — a technique about which more will be said in a moment — but it would be much easier to make piqué if all the holes had been drilled beforehand. Piqué in ivory as well as shell was carried out in Dieppe, and there is a piqué ivory box in one of the cases illustrating the "theme of tobacco" in the mu-seum in the chateau.

It is worthwhile passing in review some of the other techniques of the shell craftsman, if only because they have been little understood in the past and are, even nowadays, something of a mystery to many folk. One reason for this is that they have always been jealously guarded trade secrets. A modern British tortoiseshell worker to whom I applied for an account of his art was horrified at the mere idea of telling anyone how he carried it on. "I'm not giving away any information for lemonade," he ex-claimed, "why I was taught by me father, and he learned it from *his* father."

Whether it were intended for veneer or to make some decorative object such as snuffbox lid, tor-toiseshell was usually sawed into a thin plate. This was because it was very expensive and, as it came to the shell worker, all tied up with all the other plates, rather thick. Moreover if colors or gold foil were to be laid underneath it, they would show better if it were thin and consequently more transparent. It would also bend and weld more readily if it were thin. A curious property of tortoiseshell — which it shares with horn — is that it can be boiled until it becomes pliable, and then bent into virtually any shape. It can even be tied in a knot. Once the shell has cooled off, it hardens and retains the shape which it has been given. This property of tortoiseshell was particularly important because musical instruments which were often ornamented with tortoiseshell veneer were usually of a curving shape. Tortoise-shell veneer would follow every contour of a lute or a guitar. It would also add resonance to the music played on the instrument, and baroque in-strumentalists were just as appreciative of this quality as were the lute players of ancient Greece.

In order to render tortoiseshell soft and pliable, it was boiled in water containing salt, or heated be-fore a brazier containing "court charcoal," the kind which was burned at the English court at St. James because of its smokeless qualities. Court charcoal

German bass viol of the early eighteenth century, probably made by Joachim Tielke. It has a very elaborate tortoiseshell and ivory marquetry design on the fingerboard. Courtesy Victoria and Albert Museum, London.

had a low heat yield and was thus less likely to frizzle the expensive shell. Some tortoiseshell workers are supposed to have used potash to soften the shell. This could be made quite simply by lixiviating wood ashes; how it was applied to the shell seems to be uncertain, presumably in the hot water in which the shell was boiled.

Parts of the carapace of a turtle, such as the side pieces, are paper thin. Plates such as these, or thicker plates sawed thinner, could be molded with deeply impressed patterns, and the whole plate formed into quite a different shape, such as the bottom half of a snuffbox, for instance.

"The moulds employed for this purpose," wrote a Victorian observer, "are double, so as to contain the shell between them. Both parts of the mould being made warm, the piece of tortoiseshell, which is made warm and pliant, is placed on the lower half of the mould, and the counter-mould is closed upon the shell. The mould is then put into a press, and the upper half is gently pressed down upon the shell. The whole is then put into boiling water, and as the shell becomes more and more softened, the upper half of the mould is, from time to time, screwed down upon the shell, until at length the shell is completely pressed into the lower mould and is itself closely pressed by the upper mould, so that any devices that may have been engraved or embossed upon the two halves of the mould leave corresponding impressions upon the shell. The mould is then taken out of the hot water and steeped in cold water for a quarter of an hour, after which the shell is taken out and is found to retain the form imparted to it by the mould."

The technique of molding was to be used with splendid effect by artists such as Obrisset, who by this means formed the tops of snuffboxes or pressed out medallions. While the shell was still soft from being boiled, small gold or silver nails could be pushed into it. Once the shell was cold they would retain their position and be irremovably sunk in it. This technique was known as "nailing," or *cloué* which means the same thing in French. Ornamental shapes in gold, silver, ivory, or mother-of-pearl could also be forced into the shell, a process which was called *posé,* or "laid," shell work. Pieces of tortoiseshell could also be welded together by boiling them and then pressing them together while still hot, or by wrapping the two pieces to be joined.

the edges of which had first been pared down so that they would fit, tying paper round the overlapping edges, and then fastening it with string. The shell worker would then take a pair of tongs or pincers, rather like those used by hairdressers to curl hair, heat them, and grip the join between the two jaws of the tongs. By a variant of this method the join could be wrapped in a wet linen rag. Pincers which were not merely hot, but red hot, would then be applied to it. The heat from the pincers would turn the water in the rag into steam, which would weld the joint.

Besides the technique which I have described, the Dieppe craftsmen carved tortoiseshell with the tools which they used to cut horn and ivory, gravers, burins, and so forth. For very minute work, when, for example, they were pushing in hundreds of tiny pins to make up a *cloué* pattern, they would supple-

Detail of bass viol by Martin Voigt of Hamburg, 1726. Victoria and Albert Museum, London.

German viola da gamba of about 1580, probably made by Tielke of Hamburg. It is inlaid with mythological designs in tortoiseshell, mother-of-pearl, and ivory. Courtesy Victoria and Albert Museum, London.

ment the indifferent artificial light of the day by a condenser. This was a *boule de verre,* a glass globe filled with water, raised up on a glass pedestal. A candle would be placed on the far side of this glass globe. The rays would pass through the globe, which would act as an enormous magnifying glass, and concentrate the light on just one spot—where the carver wanted it. The Dieppe carvers probably adopted *boules* because they were used by lace-makers, and a lot of lace was made in the town. They may also have copied some of the lace-makers' designs.

Prominent among the tortoiseshell articles made in Dieppe was the tobacco box or snuff box, which had apparently originated in France. The making of tobacco boxes in pressed horn and tortoiseshell was introduced to England by French craftsmen, who had left Dieppe because of the persecution of the Huguenots in France. In 1685, out of sixty-six

Dieppe craftsmen, no fewer than 37 were Protestant. Although some recanted under the pressure of per-secution, there were probably several tortoiseshell craftsmen among the refugees who were finally allowed to leave Dieppe by ship in 1688. Among these fugitives were the parents of John Obrisset, who is probably England's best known artist in tortoiseshell. Little is known about his life, save that he was active between 1705 and 1728, and worshipped in the French church in London. He made a series of tobacco boxes and medals in both horn and tortoiseshell, several of them being royal portraits. Obrisset used to the full the peculiarly malleable properties of tortoiseshell, for example by making a cast from a silver medal, and a mold from the cast which would reproduce identical medals in tortoiseshell. To improve contemporary snuffboxes, he also took advantage of the fact that tortoiseshell is odorless and resonant. His tortoise-

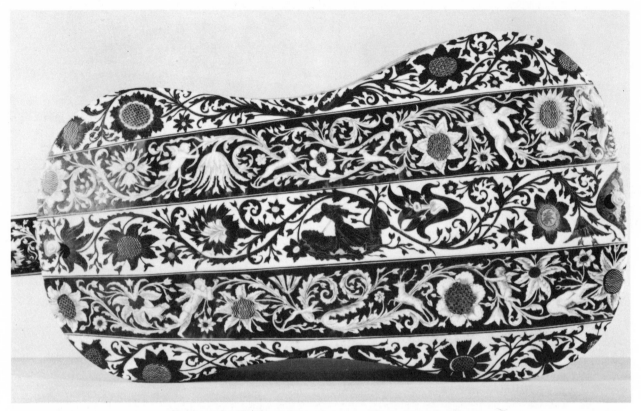

Back of the Tielke guitar. Courtesy Victoria and Albert Museum, London.

Detail of the Tielke guitar. Courtesy Victoria and Albert Museum, London.

shell boxes would not impart a metallic flavor to the snuff or tobacco they contained, and when the lid was tapped to remove any adhering grains of snuff by the user it would resound with a satisfying drumming noise. Obrisset had found it all the easier to get started in London as a horn and tortoiseshell craftsman because there had been notable English craftsmen in horn since the sixteenth century at least. Particularly conspicuous among them had been John Osborn, who worked in tortoiseshell as well as horn, and Samuel Lambelet, medalist to the Court of Brunswick Luneburg (1698-1727).

Another importation to England, via Dieppe, may have been *piqué*. This included both *cloué*, or nail designs, and *posé* designs in gold or silver forced into the shell. The former came first. It is reputed to have been invented in Naples by Laurentini around 1650, but very soon after that date it was being made in Paris. Later, as has been said, it spread to London, where for a time styles in tortoiseshell were so similar to those in France as to be indistinguishable from them. *Piqué* decoration in tortoiseshell had been confined to the use of *cloué* until the 1690s. Then flat pieces of gold, silver, and, later, mother-of-pearl began to be used. Although it has been suggested that the palmettes, C scrolls, shells, and diaper work which ornamented shell in eighteenth-century times were "tooled in" there was no need for this to have been done. It would have been sufficient to soften the shell by boiling and to press in the ornaments with some kind of clamp. Shell opens readily to receive pieces

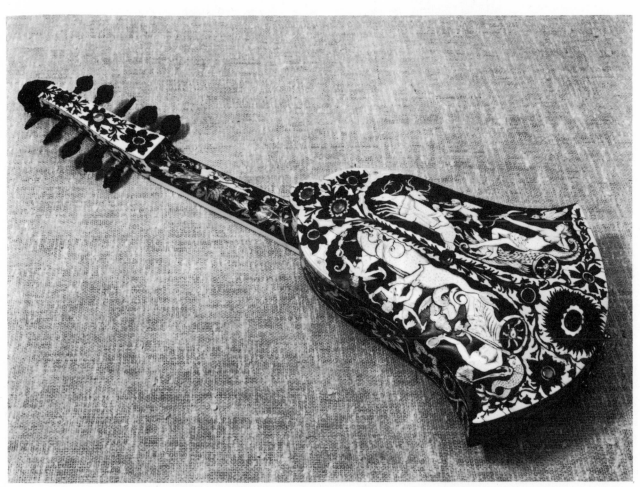

Bass viol, probably made by Joachim Tielke of Hamburg about 1700. Decorated with tortoiseshell marquetry. Courtesy Victoria and Albert Museum, London.

*Detail of viola da gamba by Tielke. Courtesy Victoria
and Albert Museum, London.*

of metal or any other insertion. The hydrogen in
the boiling water acts with the hydrogen and hy-
droxyl in the tortoiseshell to produce a hydrogen
bond. Examination of any piece of *piqué* will demonstrate that such a method of fixing is a long-
lasting one. Some pieces of *piqué* have dropped
out, it is true, but usually only as a result of bad
treatment and rough handling.

A very wide variety of objects was ornamented
in this fashion; they included watch cases, fans,
tobacco boxes, snuffboxes, patch boxes, and needle

cases. By the 1770s, *piqué* ornaments were being
made in factories and mass production of tortoiseshell ware was under way. Matthew Bolton had a
piqué factory in Soho, that part of London where
many of the Huguenot refugees from Dieppe had
settled. Fine handmade tortoiseshell work continued to be made in England right through the
nineteenth century, and it was sold at a price considerably above the factory-made ware, which continued to be produced, mainly in Birmingham.

A particular kind of *piqué* is associated with the

The Tielke guitar, Hamburg, 1693. This is the most sumptuously decorated musical instrument in the Victoria and Albert collections. Note how the maker has allowed tortoiseshell, ivory, and mother-of-pearl marquetry to speak for themselves against a sober background of ebony and light wood. Courtesy Victoria and Albert Museum, London.

Detail of the head of the Tielke Guitar. Courtesy Victoria and Albert Museum, London.

German guitar of the seventeenth century decorated with mythological designs in tortoiseshell, mother-of-pearl, and ivory. Courtesy Victoria and Albert Museum, London.

name of André Charles Boulle (1642–1732). Boulle was a brilliant French designer of furniture who began work in the royal ateliers in the Louvre in 1672. His fame rests on his daring use of inlays of tortoiseshell and brass veneer, though occasionally he used other veneers as well, such as horn, mother-of-pearl, pewter, and copper. Boulle's veneers were cut fairly thin, as anyone can see who inspects a piece of veneer from which some of the

parts of the design have been lost. He was thus able to lay one sheet of veneer on top of another in a sandwich, and saw right through them, cutting out a complicated design. The completed designs would then be applied in contrasting patterns. Brass would appear on top of tortoiseshell in one part of a cabinet, while tortoiseshell on top of brass, with the pattern reversed, would figure in another. Although Boulle had not invented this technique, his character was such a flamboyant one that certain particular methods of furniture making have become associated with his name, rather than those of lesser mortals. Nowadays almost any kind of furniture which is made from red tortoiseshell and ornamented with brass is likely to be referred to as *buhl*, after its supposed originator. Boulle rose very rapidly to fame, obtaining his first extant royal commission at the age of twenty-seven, and thereafter becoming the most distinguished cabinetmaker in Europe. Although he made vast sums by the pieces of furniture which he designed, and which were carried out under his supervision, he was always in debt and sometimes could not afford to pay his workmen, or to produce the commisions for which his patrons had paid handsomely in advance. Only his place of residence in the sancturay of the Louvre in Paris, prevented his being arrested for debt many times. He had begun life as a painter, and even when all his output lay in designs for furniture, his passion for painting continued in the form of collecting. He attended every sale, and borrowed money at exorbitant interest to buy Old Master drawings, particularly those of Raphael, for which he had an overwhelming passion. When, in 1720 his twenty workshops caught fire, he lost not merely

Two guitars: 1. Left, Altimira, mid-nineteenth century. 2. Right, Italian, mid-nineteenth century. Both are inlaid with mother-of-pearl. Courtesy Victoria and Albert Museum, London.

his seasoned raw material, appliances, models, and finished work, but forty-eight Raphael drawings and a manuscript journal by Rubens. Boulle's ambition was to create an immediate, dazzling impression of a vast, intricate design, blazing with red tortoiseshell underlaid with gold leaf or paint, brass plaques and castings, and myriads of tiny pieces of ivory, copper, ebony, pewter, and enameled metal. The effect is brilliant, the result sometimes ephemeral, as, because of the fragility of some of the raw material, many of the tiny pieces of decorative inlay have broken from the original soft whitewood core in which they were set in rather shallow recesses.

What Boulle had done for furniture was effected for musical instruments of the baroque period by a group of distinguished German craftsmen. The Tielkes of Hamburg were active in the sixteenth, seventeenth, and early eighteenth centuries, Joachim being the most famous representative of the family. Martin Voigt, who also worked in Hamburg, flourished in the early eighteenth century. Jacques Sainprae, apparently a Huguenot refugee, and therefore perhaps a Dieppois, worked in Berlin in the 1720s. The instruments which they decorated included the *viola da gamba,* the guitar, the bass viol, the cittern, and the baryton. The decoration, which was a marquetry of tortoiseshell and ivory, or of rare woods, tended to be concentrated on the fingerboard and the tailpiece, but occasionally extended over the body of the instruments as well. There is an obvious relationship between instruments decorated in this way, and those lutes, tambourines, and drums which were veneered with tortoiseshell and mother-of-pearl in India and in the Near East.

The tortoiseshell comb would also appear to have been an importation from the East. They first appear at the court of Versailles in Louis XIV's reign. The latter had very close trade and diplomatic contacts with Siam, a country with accomplished tortoiseshell craftsmen and quantities of tortoiseshell for export. Back combs may also be an Eastern importation; at any rate the back comb still worn by Sinhalese men from the coastal regions is extremely similar to the enormous back combs worn by women in the Iberian peninsula.

In England, comb making was still work for the hand craftsman until the 1830s. It had been confined to just a few districts in Yorkshire, the Midlands, and Scotland. The comb makers cut their

products from horn or tortoiseshell blanks with various kinds of saws. The largest number of combs which they could turn out in a day was about a hundred. The comb makers were "barely entitled to the name of skilled workmen; they were dissipated, unsettled, and irregular in their habits." By 1830 there were only 155 comb makers of all sorts in Scotland. In 1828, a man called Lynn invented a machine which could cut two combs out of one plate of tortoiseshell or horn. Two years later Stewart and Rowell started the biggest comb manufactory in the world, at Aberdeen, in Scotland. In their factory, tortoiseshell was cut up with a circular saw, pressed in a ram and wedge press to flatten it, and then impressed with a variety of stamped designs. The Crystal Palace, home of the Great Exhibition of 1851 in London, was a very popular pattern. The tortoiseshell then passed to the twinning machine which proceeded to cut two combs out of one slab, by sawing around the tines of the teeth, which were then pulled apart. If ladies' braid combs, or any other kinds of comb that had to be highly ornamented were being made, the sawn-out comb then passed to the hand finishers, who would smooth and round the teeth with a rasp. This operation was known as *grailing,* a word which was perhaps a reminiscence for the Dieppe term *grêle,* or rasp. The finishers would also do any kind of carving which was required. Finally the comb was polished by being buffed on a wheel covered with walrus skin. Successive wheels would be charged with compounds which the shell workers still keep as a jealously guarded secret, but which were undoubtedly powdered rotten stone, crocus powder, and powdered charcoal mixed with soft soap. These same compounds were used for polishing carved or inlaid tortoiseshell. Tortoiseshell is very easily scratched, and when hand carved the polish had to be put on by scraping it with a knife, and then with a piece of broken glass. "Glass makes a capital scraper," wrote one Victorian craft writer, "and when the edge goes off you have only to break it again and you find another. I shouldn't wonder if you found a piece of sticking-plaster handy too." The principal agent for polishing tortoiseshell was the oil or grease which was the vehicle for the polishing powders. This did not itself smooth the tortoiseshell, but it did bring up the beautiful translucent colors so characteristic of the shell. Olive oil or colza oil were used to mix the

Andromaden Perseus magno miseratus amore,
Occidit servm memoranda morte draconem.

Cum privil. Sa. Cæ. M.

HG invent. F. Saurdt sculp.
Aº 1601

C. Schonæus.

This print by the Flemish engraver Saenredan, dated
1601, symbolized the discovery of the new cameo
shells.

polishing powders. Those which I have not mentioned already included tripoli, carbonate of iron and
prepared chalk, putty powder, and bath brick.

Although "an enormous number of different patterns for combs were available [Stewart and Rowell
could supply 612 different types of braid combs
alone — these were curved combs worn in the hair]
production was so large that by the time each workman turned out his 2,000 combs a day all artistic
interest simply disappeared. The fact that stained
horn combs were made to intitate tortoiseshell so
nearly as to deceive the casual observer is another
reason why tortoiseshell carvings disappears as an
important art form during the nineteenth century.

10

The Gem from the Sea:
The Cameo

IF ONE HAD DARED TO ASK A ROMAN EMPEROR what his greatest treasure was, he would probably have replied , "my cameos,." These were not carved shells, such as those to which I shall refer in a moment, but carved *gems,* layers of differently colored onyx, sardonyx, or cornelian which had been sculpted by a lapidary so that the white part of the banded layers stood out in relief against a background of black onyx or red-brown sardonyx. People other than emperors possessed cameos, but the finest were the imperial ones, often very large gems commemorating some particular feat of an emperor, such as a triumph over the barbarians, or showing the royal imperial family grouped together.

One reason why gem cameos were very scarce, and therefore valuable, was because it was difficult to obtain pieces of banded stone of the right color and size. There was always the possibility of one of the layers "doubling" or breaking away from the rest, or showing such a faint color that it blended with, instead of standing out in strong contrast against, the rest of the carving. Making a gem was a slow, hazardous, and very expensive process. To cut the blank for the cameo took quite as much work as would all the carving and polishing that would follow. In an attempt to find a substitute for gem cameos, lapidaries started making glass ones. in which several colors of glass were fused together. Glass was brittle and would break easily, which was a great disadvantage if the cameo were set in any

object which had to be moved about, such as a chalice.

The end of the Roman Empire did not mean an end to the popularity of gem cameos. They were still in as much demand as ever, particularly by ecclesiastics, who often used them to enhance reliquaries, or church plate. In fact, the word *cameo* is first used in England by an English monk.

During the fifteenth centuries, medieval Europeans began to venture farther south, to lands where more exotic shells were to be found. Among the shells they encountered are the cowrie range, a type of shell which has a spotted *exterior,* a white *middle* ground, and a *bottom* color which could be purple, brown, blue, or gray. The cowrie had already a long history among European ornaments, because the bottom of the shell was supposed to resemble a woman's sexual parts. Hence came the association of shells with Venus, goddess of love, and also the belief that these shells were good luck charms. Any object which resembled the sexual organs of men or woman was, in antiquity, considered to be a potent amulet in putting to flight evil spirits, which are easily shocked. Anyone who wore a cowrie as an amulet might eventually find out that the colors in the exterior of the shell were arranged in layers because cowries are fairly soft, and the exterior layer might be worn away by rubbing. Medieval artists now took advantage of this pecularity of the cowrie to begin cutting cameos in its surface. It has been surmised

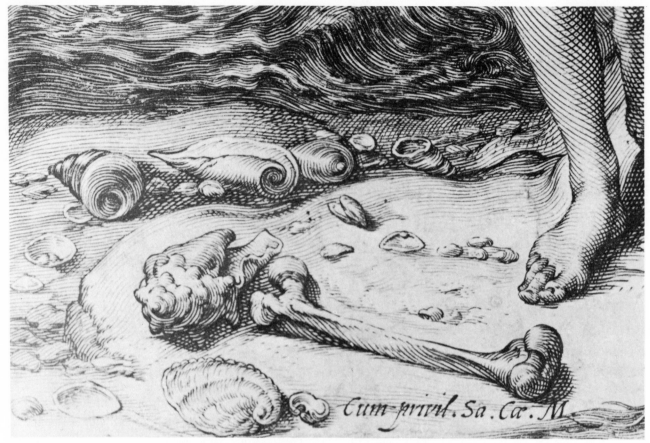

*The detail of Saenredan's print shows some of the
new shells which had begun to be imported from tropic
seas. They include a brown argonaut, turban shell, cone
shell, and horned helmet.*

that these early cameos were "cut down and backed
so as to give the ground a deep blue gray color contrasting strongly with the relief," [1] from pearl oysters,
but the ground color of a pearl oyster shell is in-
variably brown, not blue, so this surmise is unlikely
to be well founded.

These earliest shell cameos (to which the same
name as the gem cameos was applied, thus causing
confusion to many people) were mostly religious
in motif. A very fine series of them, depicting the
life of the Virgin, now in the Victoria and Albert
Museum, London, England, dates from the early
sixteenth or perhaps late fifteenth century. They may

have been used to adorn a chalice, as were the
twenty-two other shell plaques mounted on a French
silver gilt cup from the beginning of the sixteenth
century, now in the British Museum, London. The
latter series of plaques refers to one of the subjects
as Tobit. Other figures are those of Our Lord, the
Devil, St. Margaret, the Virgin, and executioner,
and angels. A number of early sixteenth century
shell cameos, this time dealing with lay subjects, are
Italian. They include carvings of Ganymede and
eagle, Hercules and Cacus, and a centaur. Because
shell cameos wear away and break fairly easily, the
earliest examples may not have come down to us at
all, and there must be many links in the chain which
have now disappeared for ever. Lord Arundel, for
example, formed a great collection of sculptures
and paintings in the seventeenth century which in-

[1]O. M. Dalton, *Catalogue of the Engraved Gems of the Post-
Classical Periods in the Department of British and Mediaeval
Antiquities and Ethnography in the British Museum* (London:
British Museum, 1915) p. xix.

cluded such items as "The Council of the Gods in Shell covered with gold; a work of great toil," and "The Triumph of Bacchus in shell covered with gold." These exhibits are now irretrievably lost, but they, and others like them, could have told us much about the infancy of the art.

It is tempting to read Benvenuto Cellini's remarks about the shell jewelery which he made in Rome as a commentary on the pioneer stages of making shell cameos. Cellini arrived in Rome for the first time in 1519.

"About this time," he wrote, "I came across some vases, or little antique urns, filled with ashes. Among the ashes I found iron rings worked in gold by the ancients, in each of which was set a little shell. I inquired of scholars, who said these rings were worn by such as did greatly desire to remain with minds unmoved in the midst of any extraordinary occurrence, whether it brought them good or evil. At the request of some gentlemen who were great friends of mine I therefore set about making some of these little rings. But I made mine of fine-tempered steel

and when they were delicately chased and inlaid with gold, they were very beautiful objects, and for making one of them I sometimes got more than forty crowns."

Forty crowns seems a large price for a ring set with a shell which was uncarved. It seems reasonable to suppose that Cellini is describing small cowries (the type of shell most likely to have been associated with a Roman burial) and that he carved them before setting them, probably with the steel garvers which he used for cutting dies for his coinage projects. I feel that it would have been foreign to the great sculptor's nature to leave anything completely unornamented, even a simple shell.

The blue and grey cowries which early Renaissance craftsmen employed had certainly been made the vehicle for some very fine carvings, in a very subdued color scheme which, however, is not without its charms. As raw material, however, cowries were very much of a stop gap. Nothing could be made from them that even remotely resembled a sardonyx cameo. The demand for gem cameos in the antique

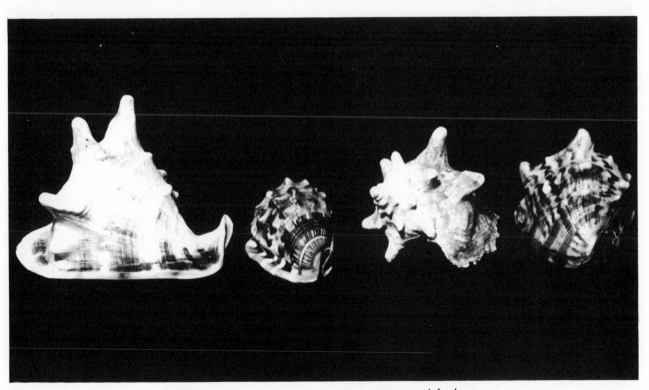

These are the very unpromising raw materials from which the cameist carves his master work. Left to right: horned helmet, red helmet, queen conch, king helmet.

*Cameos depicting scenes from the lives of Christ and
the Virgin. German, signed "F," dated 1570. Courtesy
Victoria and Albert Museum, London.*

style had become so strong that lapidaries were now
being obliged to carve German agates, or even use the
backs of ancient cameos. Avid collectors such as
Pope Paul II (1464–1471) who was so devoted
to gems that he died a martyr to his passion for
them, through having caught a cold "caused by the
multiplicity of rings exposed on his fingers," must
have looked around eagerly for some new source of
raw material for cameos.

The problem which had puzzled European amateurs and lapidaries for so long was now to be
solved for them by the American Indian. Cabeça
de Vaca, leader of a Spanish expedition which landed in Florida in 1527, published the first description
of one of the best known of the modern cameo shells,
the conches, describing how the Indians made
pendants from "the heart" or *columella,* of the shells.

The most American of these new cameo shells is the
Queen Conch, or *Strombus gigas,* from Florida and
the West Indies. This large bottom-feeding shell,
which lives on delicate algae, could, during the
early colonial period, be found just by wading out
from the beach; now it is mostly fished by skin
divers. The Queen Conch was eagerly sought by
the inhabitants of the Bahamas for its meat and for
its pink pearls. The nickname of *Conch* stuck to
them, in consequence. The Queen Conch had the
first requisite of any cameo shell, a two color structure. White cameo heads could be cut on a beautiful pink ground; unfortunately, the pink color
tended to fade.

The other new cameo shells, which soon came
into use, included the Black Helmet, or *cassis
madagascarensis,* another American shell which

came from the Caribbean. It has a white middle color and a chocolate brown ground color. The King Helmet *cassis tuberosa* also came from the Caribbean. It has a white middle color and a brown ground color, and was used as a substitute for the preceding shell. The Bull Mouth Helmet, *cypraecassis rufa,* comes from the Indian Ocean. It has a white middle color and a tawny red ground color, rather like the sardonyx of antiquity.

Of all the cameo shells, the Bull Mouth is perhaps the most often employed. The Horned Helmet, *cassis cornuta,* comes from the Indian and Pacific oceans. It had has a middle color of white on a ground color of orange; it also has a bad reputation for "doubling," that is, of the layers parting from one another.

The marriage of the classical form of the cameo and the exotic raw material of colorful shells from the East and West Indies is symbolized appropriately in a print by Johannes Saenredanus. Saenredanus, who lived and worked in the Low Countries, had never traveled, and could only have known of the new shells because he had seen them in collections. In his print, which is dated 1604, a very classical

Andromeda stands chained to a rock, waiting to be rescued by Perseus. The shells scattered at her feet are anything but classical. They include Helmet Shells, Cone Shells, Top Shells, and a Paper Nautilus.

So attractive were the new cameo shells that they secured the attention of some of the best masters, not all of who signed their work. François Duquesnoy, usually called "Fiammingo," or "The Fleming" (1594–1644), who was one of Bernini's principal rivals, was prepared to turn from his statues and ivory carvings to cut a cameo of Laocoön. By the turn of the eighteenth century, however, the disadvantages of shell cameos had begun to appear. The different layers of color might come apart in the carvings, defects, in the shape of thick cracks, could show up in the ground layers. Worst of all, the white top layer was fairly fragile, and did not keep its surface well. The worn appearance of cameos made in the previous century — a worn appearance which we can appreciate by looking at the earliest ones which have come down to us— must have convinced many sculptors that there was no point in wasting time on a material in which the

Three French sixteenth-century cameos, carved probably on cypraea shell. From left to right: Hercules killing Cacus, a winged centaur, and Hercules with the Eurymanthian boar. Courtesy British Museum, London.

art, having discovered that they could cut cameo shells with the same tools, now added them to their repertoire. Some even gave up carving the other materials and concentrated on shell.

It is not surprising that a flourishing school of cameo carvers started to develop in Trapani, in Sicily, because it had long been a center of coral carving. The first cameist there may have been Giovanni d'Anselmo, who was still at work in 1740. His artistic fortune was made when the wife of the British ambassador to Naples, Lady Hamilton, bought two of his cameos in 1769. An ivory carver of Trapani, Leonardo Bongiorno, had five assistants working for him. He also trained Gaspare Nicolini, who worked on cameos in London for the English nobility. Andrea Tipia (1725-1766) and Alberto Tipia (1732-1783) were both famous cameists, but the latter apparently confined himself just to cameos and ivory, whereas Andrea also made flowers of shell, boxes of mother-of-pearl, and Calvaries of amber. Another notable Trapanese carver was Michele Ladicina (1792-1832). After studying under Francesco Nolfo, another Trapanese, he became famous for his carvings in shell, coral, and *pietra dura*. He worked in Malta and in Rome, where he finished his studies in sculpture and won praise for his work from masters such

Scent flask, sixteenth-century Italian, formed of two cameos mounted on silver gilt. The shell used is polychrome—white, lilac, and mottled yellow, suggesting that it may be one of the cypraea shells. Courtesy British Museum, London.

finest details of their work — those on the very surface — would be the first to be worn away. Accordingly, lapidaries lost interest in shell cameos and returned instead to the cameo gems of the ancients, such as onyx and sardonyx, which were now much more readily available than they had been in the past. Coral and ivory carvers, however, who used small steel gravers and burins for their

French sixteenth-century cameo. Ganymede, seated, holds a cup from which an eagle drinks. Courtesy British Museum, London.

as Pikler and Sacchi. In Florence, where he worked for a time, he made magnificent cameos for the Grand Duke; in Vienna, he was patronized by the Imperial Court. Visits to Milan, Genoa, and Venice won him more esteem. At Naples the King, Ferdinand I, was so taken with Ladicina that he made him carve his likeness in the half bust, on foot, and on horseback. The latter part of the master's life was devoted to teaching, first in the workshop of the *Pietre Dure* of Naples, then in an art college at Palermo, and finally in the old *Accademia degli studi*, at Trapani.

During the eighteenth century Naples, and especially its suburb, Torre del Greco, developed into a cameo-carving center. The city had a tradition of shell carving going back to the Aragonese era before 1495. The great days of cameo carving began when, in 1805, Paolo Bartolomeo Martin (a native of Marseilles and a representative of a famous mercantile family there) got a rescript from King Ferdinand IV allowing him permission to set a workshop in coral at Torre del Greco, in the renaissance palace of the Marquis Carraciolo di Castellucio. Martin was granted a ten-year monopoly in the manufacture of coral, and had to keep three or four apprentices in the workshop, who must be taught his art. Martin sent to Rome for the cameo cutter Pansinette, who came to Torre del Greco, bringing with him his son-in-law, Filippo Gagliardi. The latter's children, Giovanni, Aniello, Dionira, and Rosalba, all carried on their father's art. By 1810, 200 families were working at Torre del Greco, and Martin approached the new monarch of Naples, Joachim Murat, with a request for an extension of his grant of monopoly, which was conceded on 12th November, 1810.

The incorporation of Naples in the Napoleonic Empire furthered the rise of the cameo as a popular form of jewelry throughout Europe. Everything which recalled the Roman Empire found favor with Napoleon I, who loved to be sculpted in profile so as to emphasize his supposed resemblance to the young Augustus. Cameos recalled the popular interest in the excavations going forward at Pompeii, while the soft colors of the shell carvings harmonized well with the light, gauzy draperies worn by ladies during this period. A more important consideration was that cameos were well within the purchasing power of the ordinary middle-class

patron of the period, unlike the old *pietra dura* work, the technique of which had been taught in Naples since 1738, when the *Laboratorio delle pietre dure* was set up. *Pietra dura* took a long time to produce, and was made from expensive materials, such as the Aztec jade ornaments which had been brought to Italy in Renaissance times and which, in Florence, were broken up about this period for use in the hardstone workshops.

In Naples, cameists were able to benefit from lessons given in their local school, set up in 1804, under the direction of Giovanni Mugnai. By 1833, it was being directed by Filippo Rega, born at Chieti in 1761 and trained in Naples, then subsequently at Rome in the studio of Giovanni Pikler. Cameists active in Naples during the nineteenth century included Giuseppe and Giovanni Landicina, Matteo Durante, Vincenzo Vai, Giovanni De Caro, Giovanni Finizio, Pasquale Argentino, Alberto Squadrilli, and Nicola Traversi. Masters particularly respected by the Neapolitans included Antonio Giansanti (1827-1900), who specialized in portrait work, and made the cameo cupids on the cradle which the City of Naples presented to the Royal Family of Italy on the occasion of the birth of Victor Emmanuel III. Giansanti also taught design in the Royal School of Coral, which had been set up in the city shortly after the Unification of Italy. Francesco Bruno, a Tarantese who was invited to Paris in 1902 for the celebration of the centenary of Victor Hugo, created what is surely the most original of all works in cameo, an illuminated page from Hugo's book *Les Miserables*, in which words and decoration are set in ivory, coral, lithographic stone, and shell. Giovanni Sabbato (1873-1883) sculpted a Bull Mouth Helmet, carved all over with an allegory of the greatness of England at sea, with a portrait of Queen Victoria on her imperial throne, a work which took ten years to carve. It is worth mentioning in passing that cameos were often left on the shell, and the whole shell was used as an ornament. Domenico Porzio (1853-1929) broke new ground with free and artistic compositions in the "Liberty Style" as opposed to most of his contemporaries who closely followed the antique. Other notable cameo carvers of the nineteenth century included Arcangelo Fiorillo (1847-1927), who carved mythological subjects in cameo and tortoiseshell,

Luigi Vigorito (1848-1926), Agostino Improta (1852-1929), Genarro Sorrentino (1858-1944), and Vincenzo Vitiello (1861-1938).

Not all cameists who were at work in the nineteenth century became well known. Some never sent in exhibits to the national or international exhibitions bcause they were under contract to supply their whole output to the jewelers of Torre del Greco, who shipped them to New York, London, or Paris, where they were mounted in gold or silver and sold. Of course those Neapolitans and Romans who did exhibit regularly became much better known than their home-staying contemporaries. Giuseppe Sanliani of Naples exhibited at the Dublin Exhibition of 1865. His cameos ranged in price from £2 to £4. Subjects which he exhibited included "Night and Day, the Virgin and Child, after Carlo Dolce; Flora, from the antique; Bacchanals, from a fresco found at Pompeii; Peace, Medusa, Aurora, Ceres, and other subjects." Giuseppe Tari exhibited cameos with figures of St. Paul, St. Peter, Michaelangelo, and Galileo. Luigi Sanlini of Rome also showed eighteen cameos at the same exhibition. At the Naples Maritime International Exhibition a Roman carver, Domenico Pascoli, received a first-class silver medal. Francati and Sante Maria of Rome exhibited cameos and parures carved from the Queen Conch at the Paris Exhibition of 1878.

As the nineteenth century wore on, so did the number of cameists increase. Until the century's second quarter there were no cameo cutters working outside Italy where, besides the school at Torre del Greco, there were 80 cameo cutters at Rome and 30 in Genoa in 1878. In 1852, however, an Italian cameist moved to France, and twenty-six years later there were more than 3,000 French cameists at work in the capital, making cheap, mass-produced shell carvings. Some of the Paris cameists may have been among the 7,500 Communards transported to New Caledonia and may have begun the carving of pearl shell cameos there.

As the number of artists increased, so did their status decline. Good cameos had to stand competition from cheap, mass-produced ones, made by the workman copying the same model over and over again. Some cameists at Torre del Greco had made the same cameos so often that they did not require a model, but could make the same head from memory.

Not even the imitation cameos made by Josiah Wedgwood (1730-1795)—an enterprising English potter who turned out two-colored ceramic gems which, without being exactly like real cameos, were eagerly accepted instead of them—did so much harm to cameists as this enormous over-production of their wares in cheap form. As early as 1856, only three cameo cutters bothered to advertise in *The Artistical Directory or Guide to the Studios of the Italian and Foreign Painters and Sculptors Resident in Rome, to which are Added the Principal Mosaicists and Shell Engravers*.[2]

It is significant that the cameists come right at the end of the list, as though they were a very inferior kind of art worker. Saulini Tommaso advertised that "He takes likenesses on shell or cameo. He also engraves subjects, either from ancient originals or of his composition. He was honorably mentioned at the Exhibition of London."

"Neri Paolo [a Roman] executes engravings from the best classical works of the Antiques. Among the subjects of his own composition, to be seen in his Establishment, are:

A fighting *Amazon*, on horseback.
Mazeppa, tied on the horse and hunted by the wolves in the forest.
Agar imploring water from Heaven.
The elopement of Helen with Paris.
Glaucus, Nidia, and Ione, a subject taken from Bulwer's 'Last Days of Pompeii,' at the moment of their flight from the Eruption of Vesuvius which destroyed their city."

Civilotti Carlo (a Roman) informed the public that he took likenesses in shell for brooches.

Literary sources attest the fatal facility with which cameos were produced. "In our own day," a Victorian commentator writes, "The engraving of cameos has pratically ceased to be pursued as an art." No comment on the nineteenth-century cameo, however, is so strong as the refusal of the major British museums to acquire any of that date. The Victoria and Albert Museum, London, though set up while the cameo was still a popular form of jewelry, never included any contemporary cameos in its collections. "Shell cameos, some years ago,

²Rome, 1856.

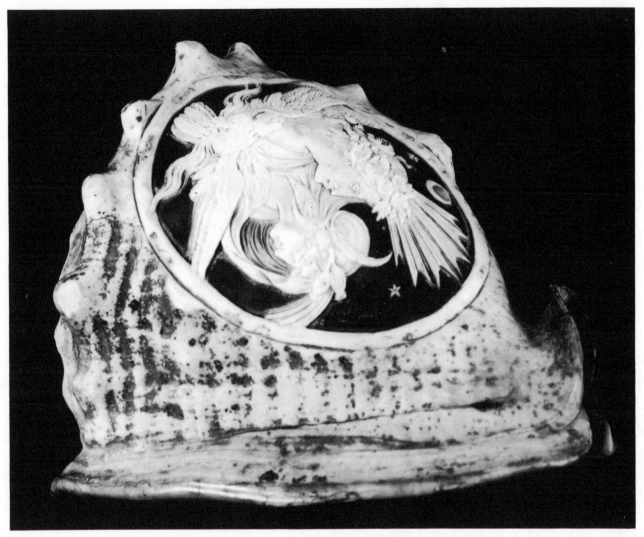

*The carver of the nineteenth-century Italian cameo left
his work on the red helmet shell on which it was cut.
Courtesy Natural Products, Kudu House, London.*

were a good deal in fashion, and even now a well-executed, artistic Roman shell cameo is an elegant work of art," commented P. L. Simmonds in 1879. Archibald Billing, however, a distinguished Victorian physician who made gem craft his hobby, wrote, "For many years the jeweler's shops have been deluged with trumpery cheap cameos, both in *pietra dura* and shell, mounted for brooches in inferior gold and sold to the million." Billing had been taught gem carving by Benedetto Pistrucci, an Italian artist who designed for the Royal Mint in London. Pistrucci must have been able to cut shell cameos because he taught Billings how to make them. The physician made several to illus-

trate a book on gem cutting called *The Science of Gems* which he published with a dedication to Queen Victoria. Pistrucci was also apparently involved with making cameos when he was stabbed in the stomach by a fellow apprentice with a *ciappola*, a sharp pointed tool which could be used in cutting gems but which was much more likely to be employed on cameo shells as the following brief account of cameo cutting technique, as it was practiced in its heyday, will suggest.

The cameist, or the director of the workshop in which he carved, began by selecting suitable shells from among the Bull Mouth and Black Helmet shells. Male shells were heavier than the female, so that these were preferred. The shell chosen had to have a good dark ground color, otherwise the cameo head would not stand out in agreeable contrast. Examples of shells carved as a whole can be found where the cameist has begun work, only to find the ground color run out and thus spoil the effect. The shells were carefully examined and marked so as to place the blanks for cameos in the parts of the shell showing the best color. A Bull Mouth might yield only a single cameo big enough for a brooch and several shirt studs, while the Black Helmet would provide five brooches and several smaller pieces.

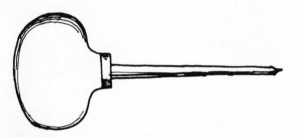

The steel chisel or graver with which nineteenth-century cameos were cut. Present-day tools are virtually identical with this one.

The whole shell was sawed up with a lapidary's slitting wheel fed with diamond dust, or, later, a saw blade fed with emery and water. A round cameo was called a *perla*, an oval one a *garbo*. These shapes were obtained from the blanks, which had originally been cut square, by grinding them with a grindstone fed with water. The edge of the cameo was rubbed down with an India stone and it was cemented to the end of a short stick with lapidary's cement made from beeswax and resin. This was built up into a mushroom shape around the cameo to secure and protect it while it was being carved. The design was now penciled onto the outside of the cameo blank. The carver had to remove the whole of the outer skin, leaving a white surface and the outside of the design, so that the head, or other subject which he was carving, was left outlined in white against a dark ground. He began by outlining his penciled sketch with a sharp-pointed tool. Next he filed away the outside of the design, and also the whole of the exterior skin. When he had done all the work he could with the

file, he began using his gravers. These were usually flat-faced, rounded, or three-cornered, though some cameists used makeshift tools like darning needles fitted in wooden handles. With the graver the cameist carved out all the contours of the face, either leaving all the edges of the figure quite square, or letting them melt into a dark background—a technique which was often used to produce charming affects, especially in landscape scenes. The projecting parts of the design were marked in black so as to prevent their being accidentally cut. Great care had to be taken so as not to cut too deeply into the ground color, which was often very thin. The completed cameo could now be lightly polished with powdered pumice rubbed on with a brush, or forced into the crevices with a shaped piece of limewood. Very little polish was required, however, because there was always the danger that parts of the design would be rubbed away.

Between the lessons in cameo cutting which Pistrucci gave to Dr. Archibald Billing, he confided the story of his life — a tumultuous one, yet probably not untypical of the cameists of the nineteenth century, many of whom, as has been seen, preferred to wander from city to city rather than settle in just one spot.

While Pistrucci was still a child, his father, an official in the Papal Courts, had been forced to flee from Rome to Bologna for fear of being executed by the French as a loyal Papal civil servant. In spite of parental disapproval, the young Pistrucci became apprenticed to a cameo carver in whose studio he was stabbed, as has been already mentioned, by a jealous fellow apprentice, who felt himself outdone by the boy prodigy. Pistrucci soon recovered and set up as a cameo carver himself. He found that he could sell every stone that he cut, but it took him rather longer to discover that unscrupulous dealers added to his work the names of long dead Greek artists and passed them off as antiques. The young cameist applied himself to his art so diligently that he began to suffer from eye trouble. The viper broth prescribed by his physician did him no good, so he set off with a friend for a tour in the Abruzzi. At Canope they stopped to watch the village women washing their clothes: "having, according to custom, taken off all their garments, and covered the body slightly with a linen cloth; so that it was a most

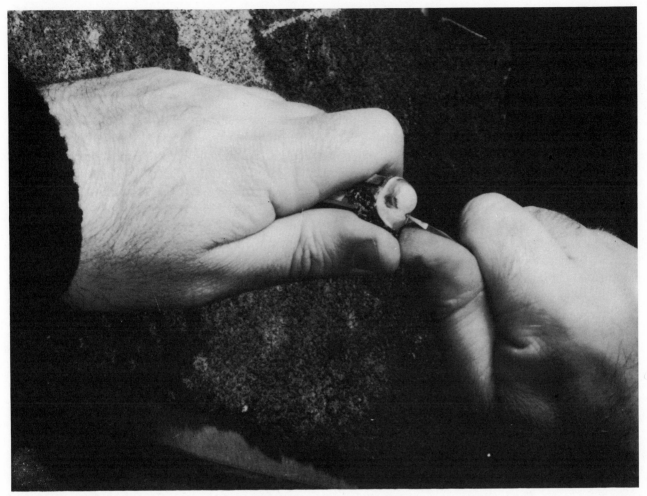

The author carving a cameo.

curious sight to behold them, within this transparent water, with their beautiful tresses, like the figures of Magna Graecia, and with ornaments of coral on their necks."[3]

Pistrucci's eye trouble disappeared as if by magic at this sight, and he had to be dragged away, protesting, by his companion, to fresh adventures. At this time the Abruzzi was being hotly contested between the French invaders and the royalist partisans. The cameist's dress, a shooting jacket of bright green, a scarlet waistcoat, a red cravat, and bushy whiskers, made the local people take him for a French officer as he passed along a road skirting high cliffs with a village perched on top of them.

The inhabitants of the place had wiped out a detachment of the French 1200 strong by pouring boiling oil on them just a short time before. Pistrucci was too good a target to miss, but fortunately there was no oil hot. As the villagers began throwing barrels down the walls of the precipice at the two travelers they spurred their horses and galloped away. It was a great relief to escape to the next village — until they found that it was held by the French, who beheaded all travelers without passports and set their heads on stakes. Pistrucci and his friend, who had no passports, escaped somehow back to Rome, where the cameo carver renewed his quarrels with fellow artists and noble patrons. When Canova failed to appoint him as one of the four professors of gem-engraving at the Academy of Rome, he left Italy forever, exclaiming, "Ungrateful country, you

[3]Archibald Billings, *The Science of Gems, Jewels, Coins and Medals* (London, 1875).

shall not have even my bones." As he landed in England, customs officers, instigated by a rascally Italian rival called Bonelli, stole all his carved gems. He spent the rest of his life in England quarreling with functionaries of the Royal Mint, who felt the English coinage should be designed by Englishmen, not foreigners, and with aristocratic English patrons who became furious when they discovered that the "Antique" gems which crooked dealers had sold them had really been carved by the clever Roman.

A physical characteristic of Pistrucci, one which had probably helped him no little in his art, was that he had very thick skin on the palms of his hands, so thick that he had to pare it from time to time with a razor. Monsignor Gaetano Garolfo comments on the horny hands of the cameo cutters of today, who live at Torre del Greco, and says that they are symbolic of their art, "an art demanding patience and taste, inspiration, and exactness."

"The Carver of Torre del Greco," he continues, "with some exceptions, is above all instinctive. He does not concern himself with theories and problems, with schools or movements. He carves well, above all those chosen subjects which allow of him

making a fine piece of work, fine more because of its impeccable finish than by its striving for effect. The secret of his artistry is bound up with the quality of the materials which he uses. These are not always easy or agreeable to work. He is at the same time the master and the slave of his material, and understands how to attend to its beauty."

In spite of valiant efforts to revitalize the cameo, such as the attempt by Professor Taverna to substitute for the helmet shells the cowries (tiger, panther, gold ringer, snake's head, money, and poached egg) so as to produce polychrome effects, it has fallen more and more into disfavor with serious sculptors. The cameists of the School of Coral at Torre del Greco produce rather stilted cameos, characterized by peculiarly tilted noses, which will not bear comparison with the fine work they do in coral. There can be no doubt that it is low water at Torre del Greco, so far as artistic cameos are concerned. The Neapolitan carvers, however, are the recipients of a shell-carving tradition that goes back to Aragonese times, and after all, low water is the time for the tide to turn.

Index